FORGET SORROW

ALSO BY BELLE YANG

The Odyssey of a Manchurian

Baba: A Return to China Upon My Father's Shoulders

FOR CHILDREN

Foo the Flying Frog of Washtub Pond

Always Come Home to Me

Hannah Is My Name

Chili-Chili-Chin-Chin

FORGET SORROW

AN ANCESTRAL TALE

BELLE YANG

W. W. Norton & Company
New York • London

For information about permission to reproduce selections
from this book, write to Permissions, W. W. Norton & Company, Inc.,
500 Fifth Avenue, New York, NY 10110

For information about special discounts for bulk purchases, please contact
W. W. Norton Special Sales at specialsales@wwnorton.com or 800-233-4830

Manufacturing by The Courier Companies, Inc.
Production manager: Andrew Marasia
Digital production manager: Joe Lops

Library of Congress Cataloging-in-Publication Data

Yang, Belle.
Forget sorrow : an ancestral tale / by Belle Yang. — 1st ed.
p. cm.
ISBN 978-0-393-06834-4
1. Yang, Belle. 2. Yang, Belle—Family.
3. Chinese American authors—Biography. I. Title.
PS3575.A53Z46 2010
813'.54—dc22
[B]
2009040993

W. W. Norton & Company, Inc.
500 Fifth Avenue, New York, N.Y. 10110
www.wwnorton.com

W. W. Norton & Company Ltd.
Castle House, 75/76 Wells Street, London W1T 3QT

1 2 3 4 5 6 7 8 9 0

To doctors
Allen B. Radner
and Dawn Mudge,
for saving my
life.

FORGET
SORROW

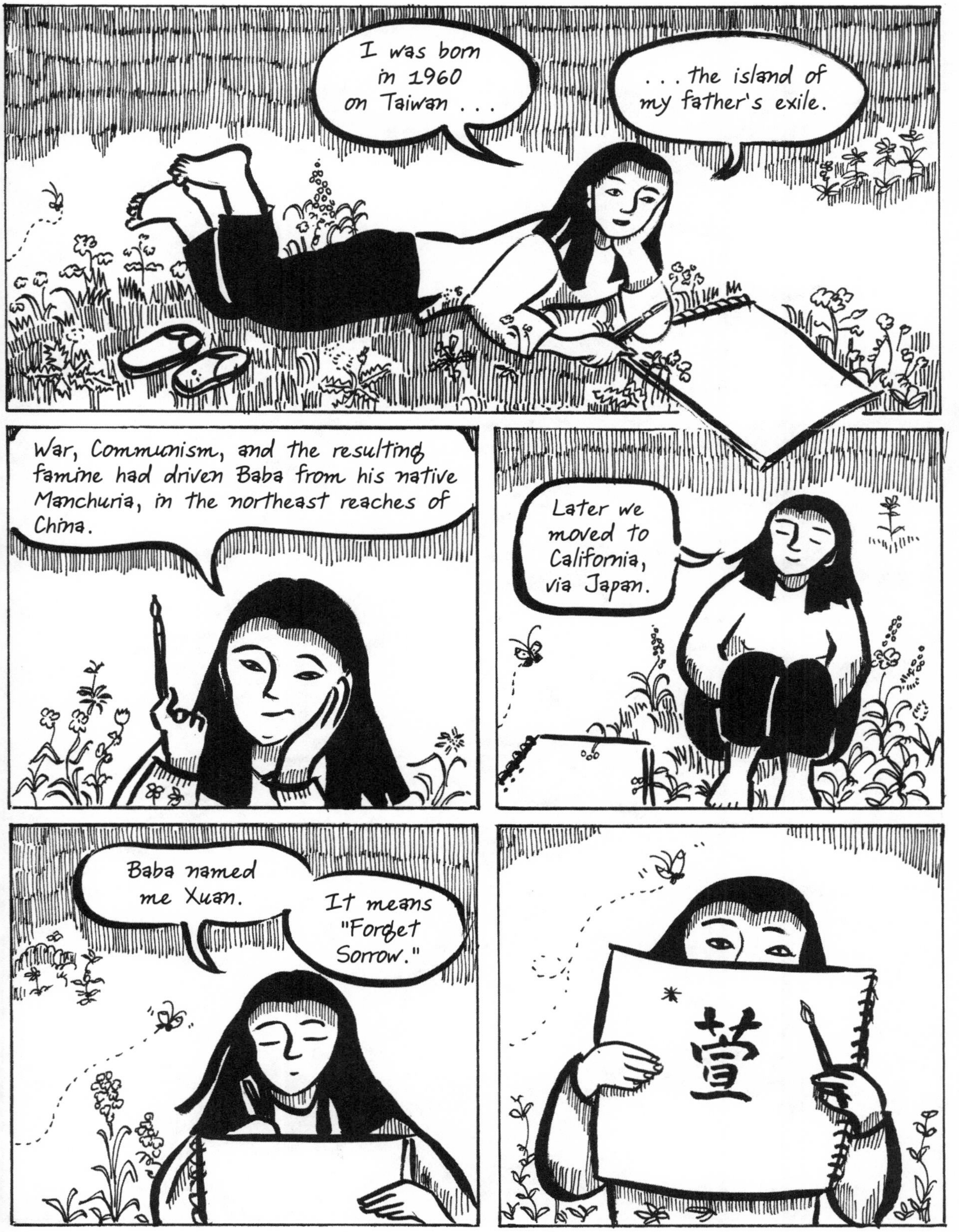
I was born in 1960 on Taiwan . . .
. . . the island of my father's exile.
War, Communism, and the resulting famine had driven Baba from his native Manchuria, in the northeast reaches of China.
Later we moved to California, via Japan.
Baba named me Xuan.
It means "Forget Sorrow."
萱

I felt an even wider gulf from my parents than most teens. My parents were not only foreign . . .

. . . they held close to their roots by immersing themselves in Eastern literature, while I studied all things Western.

The world is a dangerous place.

You must study Chinese philosophy . . .

. . . and learn to protect yourself.

What do you know? You speak broken English and don't even want to apply for credit cards.

In 1978, I set off for college.

Finally, I could breathe without my parents fretting over me.

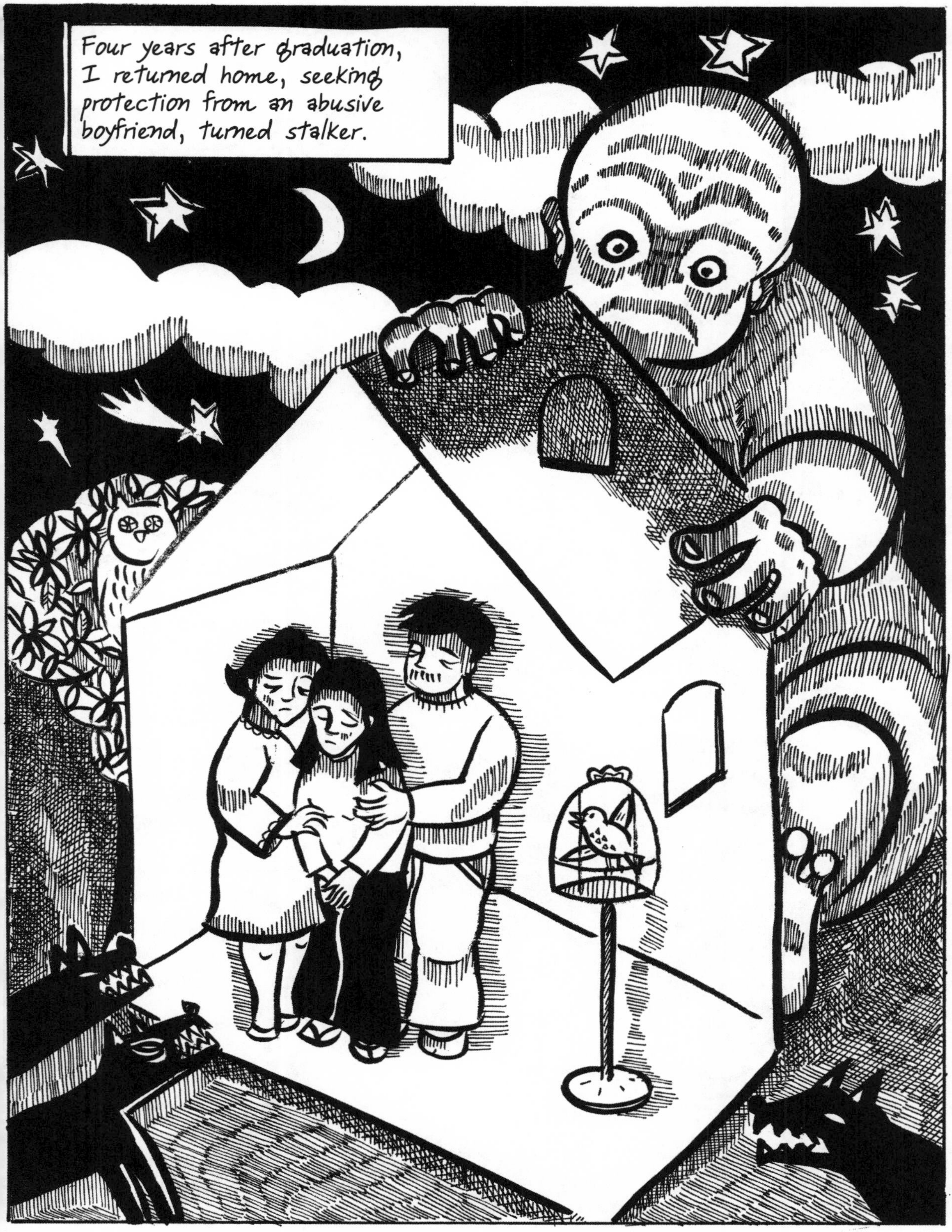
Four years after graduation, I returned home, seeking protection from an abusive boyfriend, turned stalker.

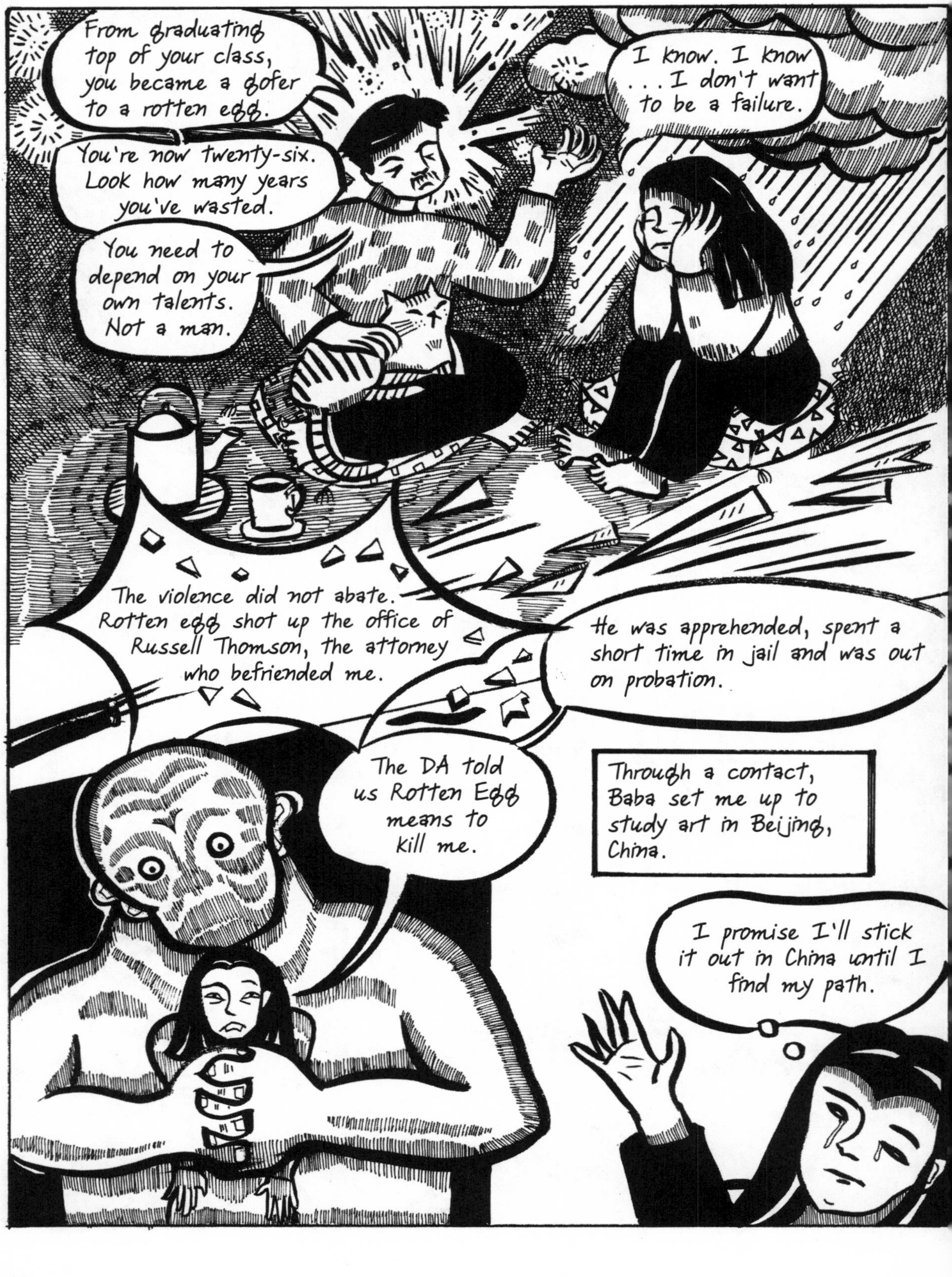
From graduating top of your class, you became a gofer to a rotten egg.
You're now twenty-six. Look how many years you've wasted.
You need to depend on your own talents. Not a man.
I know. I know . . . I don't want to be a failure.
The violence did not abate. Rotten egg shot up the office of Russell Thomson, the attorney who befriended me.
He was apprehended, spent a short time in jail and was out on probation.
The DA told us Rotten Egg means to kill me.
Through a contact, Baba set me up to study art in Beijing, China.
I promise I'll stick it out in China until I find my path.

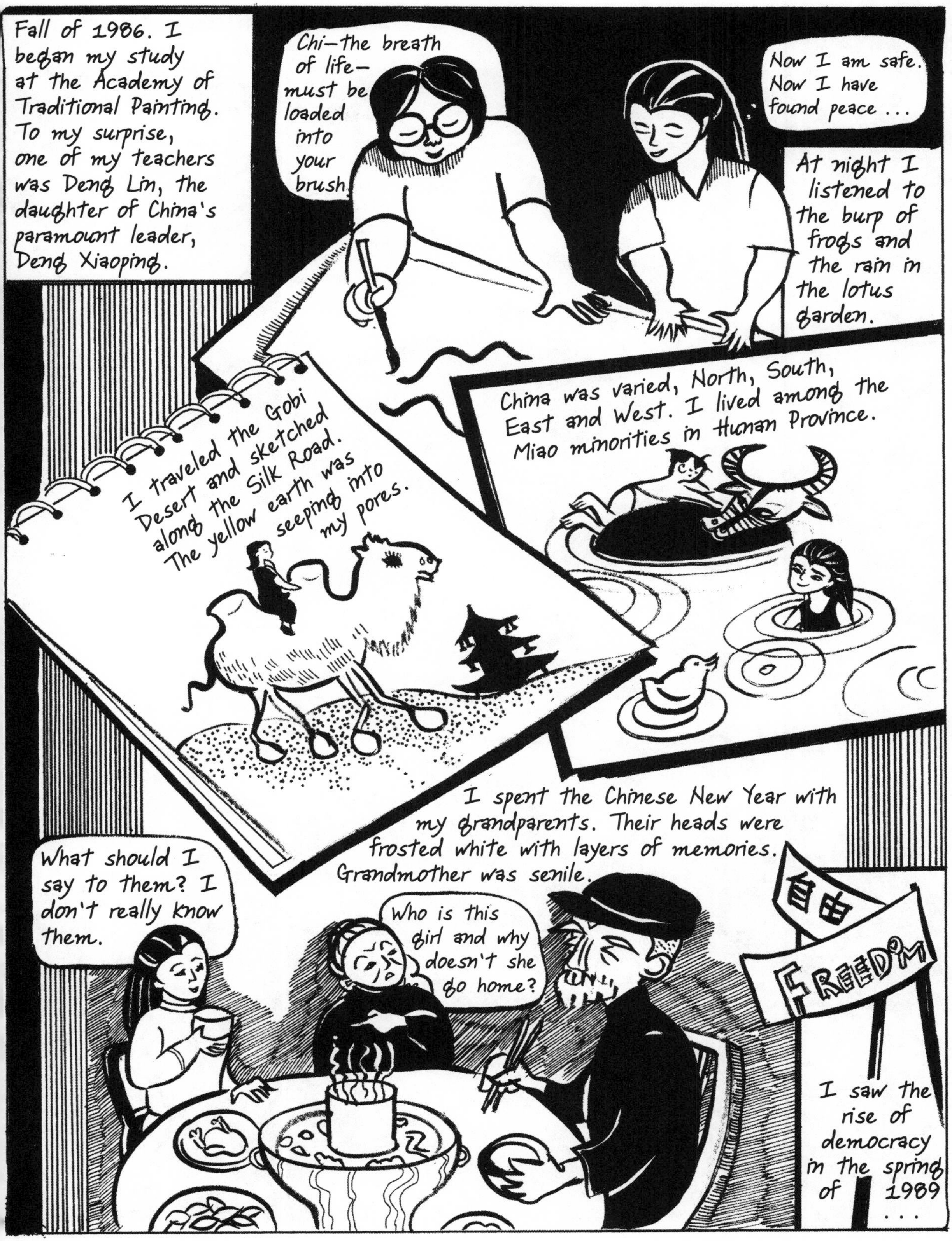
Fall of 1986. I began my study at the Academy of Traditional Painting. To my surprise, one of my teachers was Deng Lin, the daughter of China's paramount leader, Deng Xiaoping.
Chi—the breath of life—must be loaded into your brush.
Now I am safe. Now I have found peace . . .
At night I listened to the burp of frogs and the rain in the lotus garden.
I traveled the Gobi Desert and sketched along the Silk Road. The yellow earth was seeping into my pores.
China was varied, North, South, East and West. I lived among the Miao minorities in Hunan Province.
I spent the Chinese New Year with my grandparents. Their heads were frosted white with layers of memories. Grandmother was senile.
What should I say to them? I don't really know them.
Who is this girl and why doesn't she go home?
自由
FREEDOM
I saw the rise of democracy in the spring of 1989 . . .

The people of Beijing demanded an end to corruption. They wanted participation in government.

I was at the CBS headquarters that night and was invited to translate for dissident Fang Lizhi and his wife.

They stared numbly at the patterns in the carpet.

They were seeking safety from government persecution and certain arrest.

I wish I could help them and comfort them.

I wish I could ask Deng Lin to tell her father to stop the violence.

But I would not see her again, since I had finished my program at the academy.

All that summer, there was a palpable pall over the city.

I found work at the American Embassy. At night, I translated news for United Press International.

Soldiers are giving free haircuts to citizens . . .
Twenty thugs were executed . . .
The price of tomatoes is 85 mao per jin . . .

One night, I was dragged out of my taxi to have my passport seized.

The first Chinese who left for America wanted their bones returned to China, but I was scared I'd die in China, my bones never returned to America.

FEDEX HOME

On October 7, 1989, I returned to California. I felt lucky and guilty that as an American, I was free to leave the devastation behind me.

北京 BEIJING

I did not find my path in China as I promised. I am returning as bedraggled as I was when I fled home three years ago.

Rotten Egg stole the contents of our trash bin after the Tiananmen Massacre, looking for evidence of your return.

Stay home a year and practice your calligraphy. You'll reach a level of peace many layers deep.

Yes, then you'll know just what you need to do.

I am nearly thirty, what future can there be in practicing Chinese calligraphy here in this cold garage?

My parents' words would prove true.

One dark and stormy night, when the power went out, I got into my parents' big bed to stay warm.

Can you tell me more about our family in Manchuria, Baba?

Chairman Mao, are you here to listen, too?

Let's begin in the winter of 1944, on New Year's Day, when my father and his three brothers were reunited at the house of Yang, my grandfather's estate in Xinmin.*

新民 *Xinmin means "New People."

Good fortune was rare, now twelve years into the Japanese occupation of Manchuria. The Japanese had invaded in 1931, then in 1937 used Manchuria as a springboard to attack China south of the Great Wall.

In the summer of 1943, Americans based in southern China had bombed the Japanese occupied areas of Manchuria where two of my uncles lived.

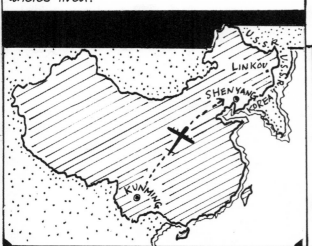

People were in a panic. My uncles fled with their families to Xinmin.

So my father and three uncles were together again for the first time in years.

Eldest Brother, let's go to the old kiln and take a look around.

Good idea, Number Two, we played there when we were kids.

Number Four, let's join them.

Why not, Third Brother?

my father

Grandfather seemed particularly satisfied.

Look at my four fine lads . . .

The other branches had an earlier start. If we work just as hard, there is no telling what my sons will accomplish.

In a few decades, his branch of the Yang clan had climbed from farming to become scholars.

The other branches had attained power and fortune. Their sons had become officials during the last dynasty and under the Republic.

Sun Yat-sen, father of the Republic

Grandfather waved to me, signaling me inside to see him.

My heart was beating fast. It was an honor to be invited into Grandfather's chamber.

Zu-Wu,* winter and summer, you keep scooting out to Shantuozi. Have you ever climbed Granddaddy Hill?

*祖武

*Zu-Wu means "Ancestral Warrior."

Oh, I've been up there lots of times. Looking down when the sorghum has been cut, the land is so big, it's as if I'm riding on the shoulder of a giant.

Well, you are certainly a poet.

Come sit here with me.

Zu-Wu, we must understand the past so that we may understand how we became who we are today.

Our ancestor, the very first Yang who came to Manchuria, is buried on top of Granddaddy Hill. That was eight generations ago. Someday I will rest there, too.

This past summer, I had been on top of Granddaddy Hill. I had climbed the cypresses and looted crows' nests for their blue eggs. Grandfather would have thought it disrespectful to the ancestral graves.

Toward the end of the reign of the Qianlong emperor, in the last decade of the eighteenth century, a young man from the Big Village of the Yang Clan near Xi'an . . .

Killed a tax collector . . .

with a hoe.

Yang fled east. He came to Tongguan where the Yellow River, as it spills south from Inner Mongolia, suddenly veers east.

From there he wandered east into Henan Province and then inched north into Hebei, working as a laborer on farms dotting the way.

Many years later, he came to Changli, just south of where the Great Wall meets the sea.

They say a man without family is without value, because he is responsible to no one. He married a farmer's daughter.

In a year of drought and famine, he left with his wife and two sons . . .

for the rich soil beyond the Great Wall, which had never been put under the plow.

The family advanced ten li* a day into terrain of dunes, scrub willows and wolves.

*One "li" is a third of a mile.

21

They rested in hamlets, staying a week to several months to help in the fields.

In winter, farm families were grateful for their help in making hoes, fixing trappings, clearing snow, sharpening saws and axes, pounding out the plowshares.

No, can't stay.

We want to have a go at our own place, too.

For years the small family toiled northward, finally arriving in the region northwest of the Willow River.

Seems workable here.

I hope so. There's no going back.

They had come to Shantuozi, "Hamlet of the Shan Clan," but it was no longer home to even half a Shan. The people must have been driven elsewhere by fresh needs.

They liked the smooth, round hill in the middle of Shantuozi, which stood out for miles around.

It seemed a shoulder to lean on and sheltered them from the wind blowing out of Mongolia.

Later generations would call it Granddaddy Hill. At the foot of the hill, they raised a mud cottage and laid claim to the surrounding land.

The soil was generous. In time, Yang the fugitive had become the elder of his clan.

At the foot of the bald hill, brick houses sprang up in neat rows, each household headed by a male of the Yang clan.

With their rise to moderate wealth, the Yangs had the means to school their children.

Two great-grandsons went on to pass the imperial examinations and served the emperor in Beijing.

With prominent men in the family as new members of the scholar-gentry class, the clan history needed a bit of improvement.

But before the revisions could be made, it was necessary to upgrade the Yang family burial grounds.

Only then can the imperial officials be able to point proudly to their great-grandparents' graves and say, we are so-and-so from an established family.

Not butchers of pigs and opera singers, the dregs of Chinese society.

They might even boast that they were descendants of the Sui emperors in Xi'an, whose surnames were Yang, but under no circumstance would they mention that their great forebear had blood on his hands.

Yet what emperor did not lob off a head here and there to become and remain emperor?

A geomancer was invited to make improvements.

This spot is well endowed with fengshui.* Ancestral burial ground with good fengshui promotes future generations of talent. Best of all, it will never treat the ancestral bones to a soaking.

*Wind and water.

There, at the crown of the hill, the grave mounds of the first Yang and his wife were neatly enclosed with a wall that came to encompass five *mu* of land.*

*A "mu" is about a third of an acre.

Trees were planted just inside—poplars, willows and cypresses—which soon grew into giants, casting inky shadows.

The officials in Beijing announced a visit to the site every three years. They made the arduous travel of over half a month by wagon.

In preparation for the visit, weeds were plucked from the grave mounds, and pigs were slaughtered. Incense and money for the dead were burned.

On the long-awaited day, the peasants from the surrounding countryside gathered along the roadside to watch the colorful procession.

The officials wore vermillion hats that trailed long peacock feathers and flowing Manchu-style gowns of office.

They made their way up the hill to the grave mound of the Great Ancestor, the symbolic heart of the clan.

Their full kowtows proclaimed: we are men who deeply respect our past, therefore, ourselves. We will do nothing to disrupt the harmony of the universe and shame ourselves before our ancestors.

And this was the way we came to Man-churia eight generations ago.

But family history is not the reason I invited you here today.

You can help me copy this rare Willow Forest Taoist Scripture, a discourse on achieving enlightenment through meditation. Come here in the afternoons.

You can trust me, sir.

I felt proud to be asked by Grandfather.

It was time to go, but I had a favor to ask of Grandmother. She had been seated across the room.

Grandma, see Zu-wu's eyes rolling round and round? This rascal knows exactly what's what.

Mmmm ...

She was a dour nub of a woman with narrow eyes.

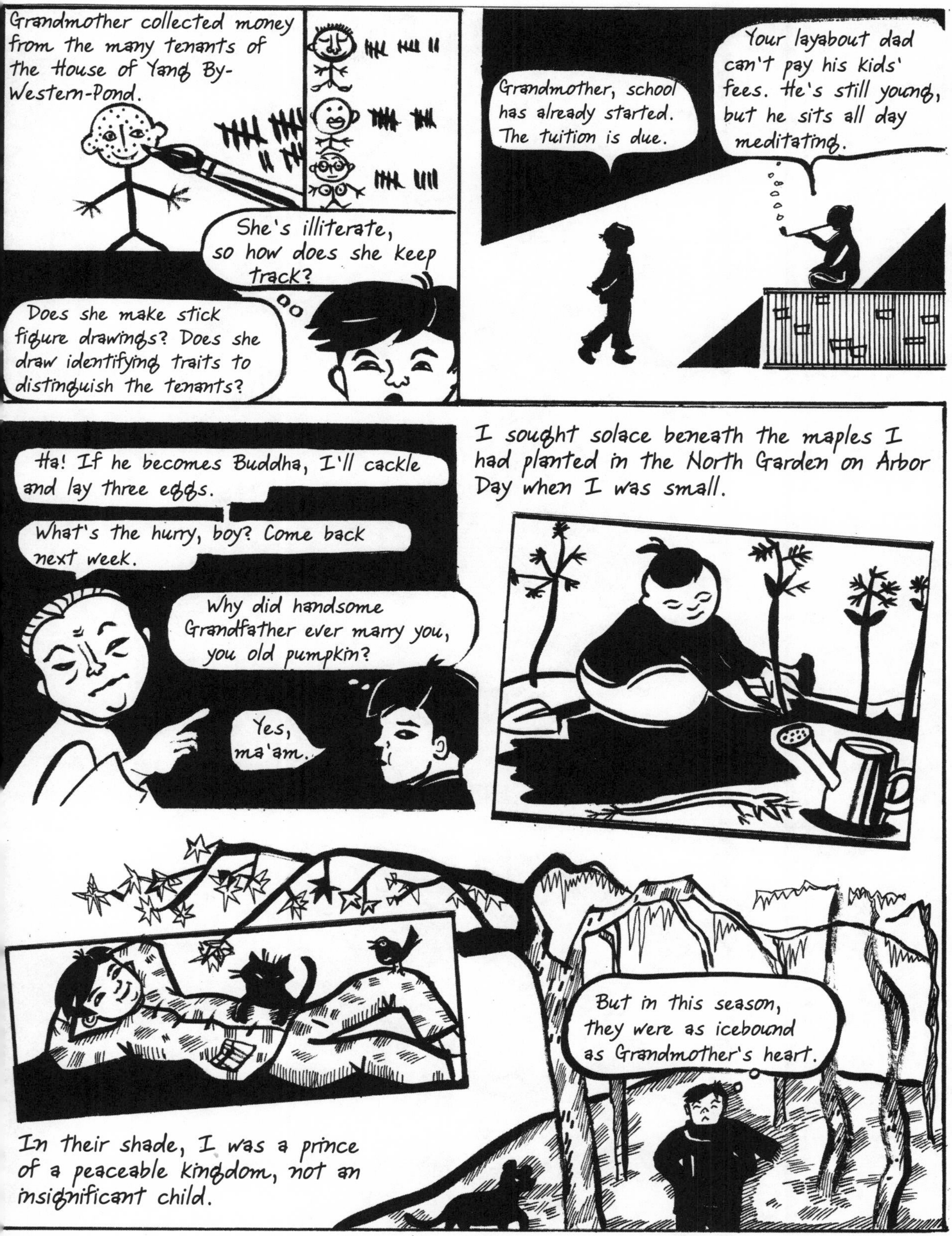
Grandmother collected money from the many tenants of the House of Yang By-Western-Pond.
She's illiterate, so how does she keep track?
Does she make stick figure drawings? Does she draw identifying traits to distinguish the tenants?
Grandmother, school has already started. The tuition is due.
Your layabout dad can't pay his kids' fees. He's still young, but he sits all day meditating.
Ha! If he becomes Buddha, I'll cackle and lay three eggs.
What's the hurry, boy? Come back next week.
Why did handsome Grandfather ever marry you, you old pumpkin?
Yes, ma'am.
I sought solace beneath the maples I had planted in the North Garden on Arbor Day when I was small.
In their shade, I was a prince of a peaceable kingdom, not an insignificant child.
But in this season, they were as icebound as Grandmother's heart.

黄花高士節

After school one day, I tiptoed into Grandfather's room and began copying the Taoist scripture.

Grandfather was meditating.

Grandmother did finally pay my tuition.

That afternoon, the nurse from the House of Bai came to visit.

Haaiii . . .

Your second daughter's taken a turn for the worse.

If Second Aunt can make it through this winter . . . when the forsythia is in bloom, I know she will get better.

Of my three aunts, I loved Second Aunt best. She rarely laughed deeply from the belly, only slightly in the corners of her mouth.

I loved the fragrance of herbs cast from her clothes and hair.

I remember when the matchmaker found her a prospective groom. Second Aunt had prepared all morning on the day of the mutual inspection.

She snatched a shy eyeful of the young man and withdrew. It would have been improper to exchange a hello.

I followed Second Aunt into the back room. Her cheeks were the color of boiled prawns. She looked ready to laugh, ready to cry.

Well, did you like what you saw?

But Grandmother had already decided against the young man.

Humnph. He can't sit still. Just like a doubengzi.* He's no steady character.

*A flea jumping on the back of a dog.

Soon after, the matchmaker produced a young man named Bai. Second Aunt said she preferred to keep out of sight.

29

Grandmother deemed Bai honest and approved the match.

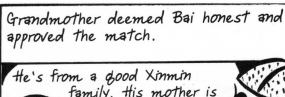

He's from a good Xinmin family. His mother is dead, so our girl won't have to serve a mother-in-law.

*double happiness

A little after the marriage, Bai's work took him to faraway Changcun. Second Aunt stayed behind to take care of her in-laws. Soon gossip reached the House of Yang: Bai was keeping a mistress in Changcun.

You may know a man's face but you can't know his heart.

Second Aunt joined Bai in the north, but her husband's affair did not end. She returned to the House of Bai. Grandfather went to see her.

Come home, daughter.

I can't. I have his child.

A boy was born to the House of Bai.

When the baby was six months old, Second Aunt started to cough up blood.

She was treated with Western medicines. Then Chinese herbal remedies. When these failed, in desperation, a shaman was invited.

A great sadness hung in the room after the nurse from the House of Bai had departed.

I decided to visit Second Aunt. She'd always had unspoken sympathy for her nephews, who bore the brunt of the elders' rage.

You can hide in my room, little one, till your father cools down.

Waaa! Dad hit me with his pipe.

But I had no money to buy her a gift. Even if I did, there was not much to purchase given the steely Japanese grip over commerce. I headed for the barn to see if the hens had laid any eggs.

Feeling inside the nests—fashioned from coils of thick rope, strung on horizontal poles—I found four and put them in my pockets.

First, I sprinkled a handful of grain in the yard, so the chickens would not make a fuss at my theft.

The Bais had recently moved to the western part of Xinmin.

I found my aunt, sitting on the kang* huddled over a brazier. She seemed unable to keep warm.

Auntie, you're so skinny.

I'm fine. I'll get fat in a hurry.

* Sleeping platform with hot air beneath piped in from the kitchen.

I wish I had something nicer to give her.

Where did you nab those, eh?

Our barn.

Zuwu, you are borrowing flowers to honor Buddha.

For the life of me, I could not muster another shred of conversation.

Zuwu, tell your ma your aunt is doing well.

Next time you come, there's no need for you to rob the hens, d'you hear?

I won't find any more, Aunt. It's getting cold. The hens will soon be laying nuggets of ice.

32

Before the forsythias could bloom, Second Aunt died. Because she had died young, not as a great matriarch, her funeral was to be a quiet affair, sans banquet.

I was too insignificant to join the funeral procession.

The modest casket of unlacquered wood rested in the first wagon.

It was the son's duty to direct his mother's soul to nirvana.

The ground was crusted with ice and crunched with the passage of the wagons. I hated Bai's calm and the ruddiness of his cheeks.

You killed Second Aunt, not the tuberculosis. You made her so sad, she festered inside and died.

Grandfather was the sole representative from the House of Yang. His face betrayed no emotion.

No, thank you. I'd rather follow on foot.

I followed the procession at a distance.

What is Grandfather thinking and feeling?

After covering a few li, Bai's father climbed out of the wagon.

Venerable Yang Junchen, you should go home and rest. The Bais have all gathered. We will not let your daughter go alone.

I would like to accompany my child a little farther.

As the procession approached Xinmin's Western Gate, I gained on them. It was then that Grandfather noticed me.

Ah, you've come, Zuwu!

His tired, gentle voice broke my heart.

So, you're also here to send off your aunt.

You may represent the House of Yang. Granddad needs to rest.

Yes, sir.

How can I make you feel happy again, Grandfather?

34

I was now under official orders to accompany my aunt. I felt grown up. I scrambled to catch up.

When I turned around, Grandfather was still standing in the middle of the road, watching. Farther on, I turned again and saw the old man slowly walking away.

When I looked back a third time, Grandfather was looking over his shoulders, too, for one last good-bye to his daughter.

Shortly, the procession passed through the Western Gate. I slowed my steps and bid my aunt a silent farewell. The Bais would bury her in their family plot.

When the cortege disappeared completely behind the dunes, I could still hear the spirit banner flapping.

When the spirit banner finally vanished, I stopped and savored the silence that engulfed me. The dunes glistened, and the piles of snow against their northern slopes made everything look fresh, light, and young.

Once I was home, I wanted to tell Grandfather that I had fulfilled my duty and had accompanied my aunt beyond the Western Gate.

But when I opened the door to his apartment, the fragrance of incense was the smell of grief. I did not have the heart to go in.

The gray-haired should not be burying a head of glossy black. But this was only the beginning of the end of the natural order of things for my family.

My aunt had completely disappeared like a puff of warm breath against the north wind.

Sigh. Was your second aunt Grandfather's favorite too?

The power came back.

He loved all three of his daughters but especially my second aunt's quiet, devoted ways.

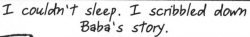

I couldn't sleep. I scribbled down Baba's story.

Two days later, I showed him my typewritten pages.

Here, illogical.

I hate that nasal tone.

This wrong, too.

Tsk. You're such a killjoy, Baba.

Me, Killjoy?

We bring you to America for education. You find Rotten Egg stalker boyfriend!

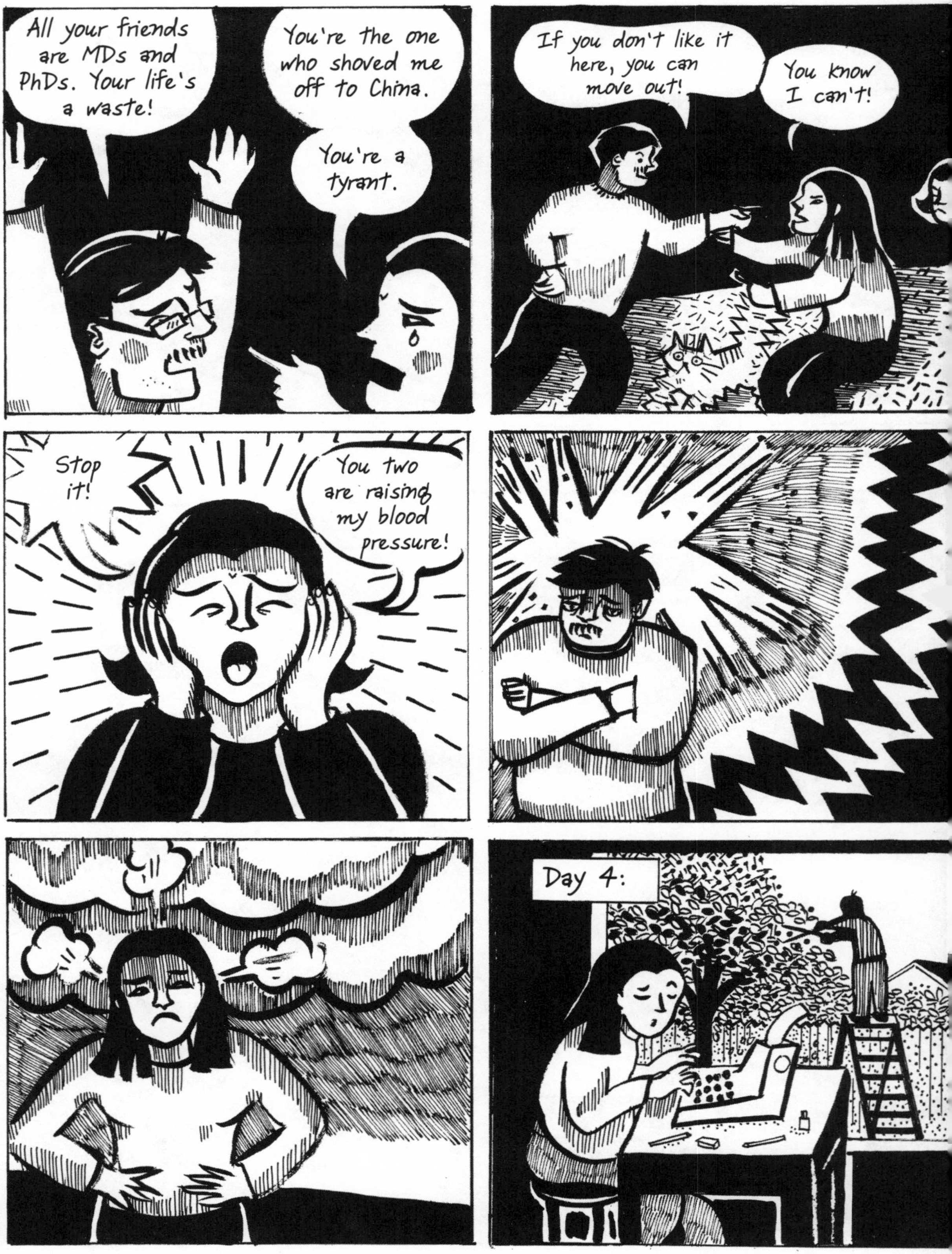
All your friends are MDs and PhDs. Your life's a waste!
You're the one who shoved me off to China.
You're a tyrant.
If you don't like it here, you can move out!
You know I can't!
Stop it!
You two are raising my blood pressure!
Day 4:

I love Baba's stories.

I want to be able to give voice to people who were forgotten.

Rotten Egg silenced me with his fist when I disagreed.

The Chinese government silenced its citizens with tanks.

I have a voice in America. I won't waste it.

Rotten Egg has reduced my world to these four walls, but I won't let him waste my life.

I'm going to work with Baba until I put in the last period . . .

and send it out into the world.

Mmph.

Baba! Are you okay?

How embarrassing if our neighbor found me sprawled on her side of the fence.

I'm glad you're okay.

I've rewritten the story, Baba.

Here you go. I read it. It's good.

Thanks, Ma.

Much better. Now logical.

Tell me more, Baba.

Yes, let's pick up where we left off... my grandparents were grieving...

Grandfather lingered on the garden bridge, which spanned a trench of water, now frozen.

In the springs past, the reeds that had grown out of the mud bore white, tassel-like flowers.

From the bridge, Grandfather watched returning swallows swoop after insects.

I warn you. You'll go blind if one of them falls out!

We kids poked the swallows' nests under the eaves, to get a better look at the babies.

On summer afternoons after a squall, the trench filled with water. Everything glistened with raindrops.

Now in winter, what was he thinking?

Was he remembering his youth?

Was he recalling the year his elder brother lost the family land in a game of dice?

Why is Second Brother going away?

I'm hungry.

He was forced to quit school. His impoverished, widowed mother had sent him, in the dead of night, from their home in Shantuozi to become an apprentice at a grain brokerage in Xinmin City.

There he had been employed to wash chamber pots and spittoons, draw water, sweep the floors, shovel snow, and pour tea for his bosses. He always sent the money he earned to his mother.

When they saw that he was very bright, they put him in the accounting office and taught him the use of an abacus.

At age seventeen, he was promoted to sales representative. Wherever he traveled, he was entertained lavishly by clients who wanted a good price.

Gan bei!*

* Bottoms up!

At twenty, he quit his job, took out loans and went into grain brokering for himself in Xinmin.

But his start-up could not compete with the old, established brokerages. He made no money, and in his tenth year he nearly lost everything.

As they say, the pressure's so bad, my eyes are going to turn blue.

He was saved by an old friend who worked under the Manchurian warlord Zhang Zuolin. He was allowed to borrow as much as he needed from the Bank of Manchuria.

I'm trusting you. Don't make me a fool.

I'll repay you with interest.

Zhang Zuolin began his career as a bandit. After the fall of the Qing Dynasty in 1911, he ruled Manchuria like a king until the Japanese assassinated him in 1928.

Grandfather's business prospered. He bought back all the land his brother had lost. He also bought a large estate in Xinmin.

People in the region heard about the wealth of the House of Yang By-Western-Pond in Xinmin. Unfortunately, so did the bandits—the red beards, as they were called. (I do not know why: perhaps long ago, invading Turkic barbarians of the steppes had red beards?)

Fire!

The red beards had been studying the compound for years trying to find a way inside. One night they started a fire.

The buildings were of brick, which no bullet could pierce. Square holes had been built in the walls through which to shoot at marauders.

Stay inside! It's a ploy to get us to open the gates.

Once they come over the wall, open fire. But shoot over their heads. We want to scare 'em, not kill 'em.

Suddenly a strange scratching noise came from the South Gate, accompanied by a strange whimpering, like a dog begging to be let in.

All the family dogs came to the window, but the sound continued...

Grandfather realized the red beards were sawing on the gate!

The tenant nicknamed Pockmarks could not stand the tension any longer.

I'll kill you sons of bitches!

Sons of Bitches! Settin' fire and burnin' my nest.

Grrr

Who's afraid of a few farm tools, eh, boys?

Pockmarks, get the hell inside! My bullets won't know the difference between you and a bandit!

Ai-ya!

BANG Piang! PIANG Pow!

When a man becomes wealthy, it is not only the bandits who keep him in mind night and day. Grandfather gave generously to the renovation of Buddhist temples.

In the morning, a carpenter and a smith came to strengthen the double panels of the South Gate.

Corners wrapped in iron

Follow Buddha so you will not be recycled as a dog, a worm or even as a human being.

Each fall Yuan the Idiot, a Taoist beggar, came for winter clothes. Yuan taught Grandfather meditation to still the heart.

Your problems are like your shadow.

The faster you run from your shadow, the faster it runs after you.

But if you rest in the shade, your shadow disappears.

Your grandfather and this beggar became friends?

Yes, Grandfather had all he wanted, including prestige and power, but only with Yuan could he speak his mind freely.

Every year, when the frost was upon the eggplant, Idiot Yuan arrived.

Come in. Come in, dear friend.

Eh, Granddaddy, the steely winds of autumn are again upon us.

I have a coat and a wadded jacket and trousers to see you through winter.

By summer, Idiot Yuan would have sold them.

Together the two men talked for hours, delving into the mystery of the Tao.

Why does Grandfather always invite this man?

47

As Idiot Yuan spoke, his arm plunged down the collar of his jacket . . .

He's so filthy.

and plucked out a louse, and put it under his cap.

Why did you put it there? Why didn't you smash it with your fingernails?

That varmint will have trouble acclimating to the water and soil of its new home . . .

. . . and will die a most peaceful, natural death.

HA HA Ha ha HA Ha ha ha Ha ha ha

!!!

Sometimes the two men sat silently facing one another, their eyes closed. They were conversing spirit-to-spirit. What remained of their bodies were mere husks.

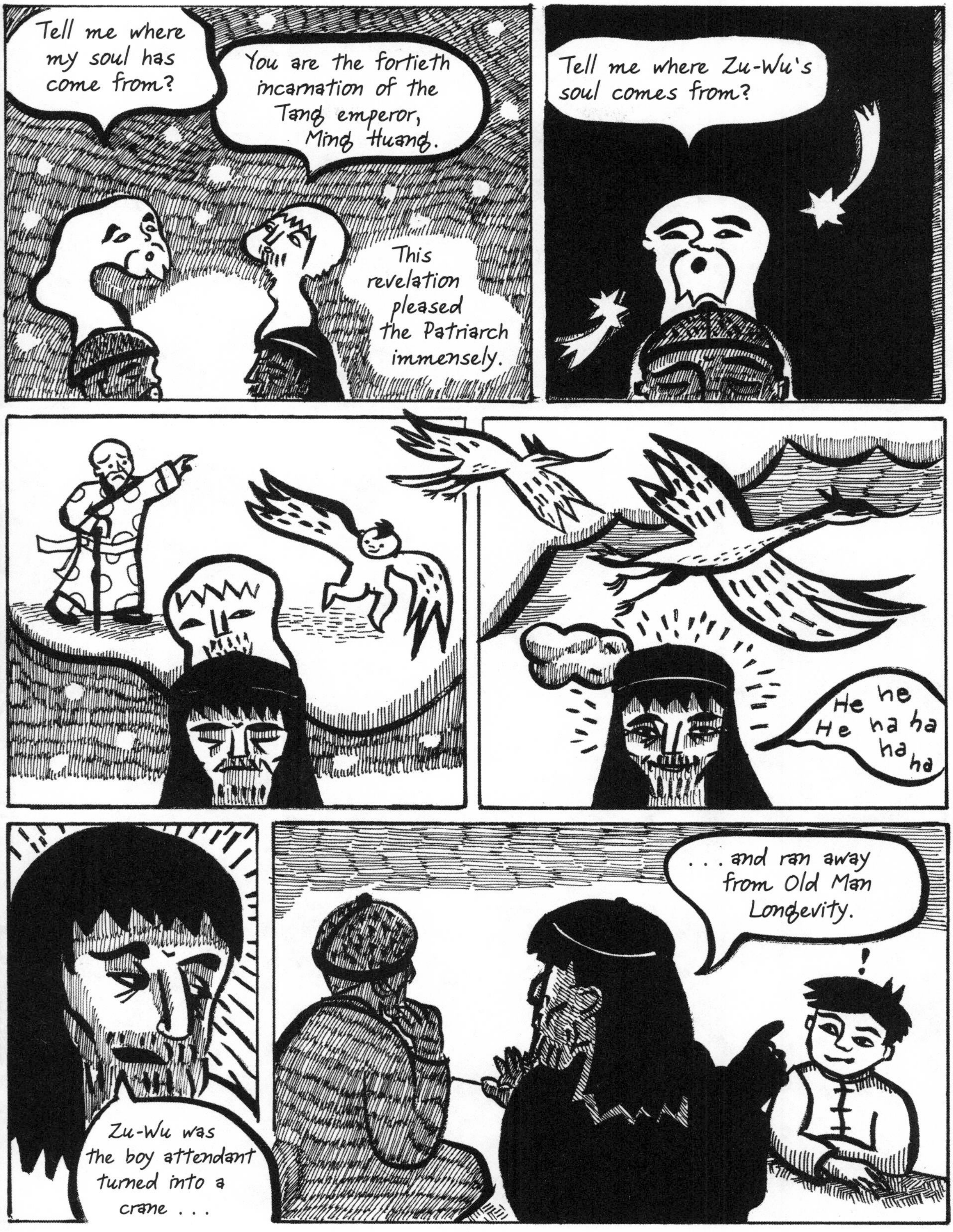
Tell me where my soul has come from?
You are the fortieth incarnation of the Tang emperor, Ming Huang.
This revelation pleased the Patriarch immensely.
Tell me where Zu-Wu's soul comes from?
He he He ha ha ha ha ha
Zu-Wu was the boy attendant turned into a crane . . .
. . . and ran away from Old Man Longevity.
!

Is this the reason why you use "Flying Crane" as your pen name?

Why, yes.

Not only could Yuan see the past, he could see the future.

Old Granddaddy, last night when the Three Stars* were directly overhead at midnight, I saw the gates of Hell busted down . . .

*Orion's Belt.

. . . and all the hungry ghosts come pouring out.

Surrender all earthly illusions. Relinquish everything! Be rid of the wealth that will be your bane!

The old ways will disappear. There will be chaos. Relationships will be perverted. Heaven and earth will be turned upside down. Rulers will be killed. Sons will betray fathers.

Baba, what did your grandfather think of the prophesy?

MROW

He believed Yuan, but he was wealthy, his house securely established. He wanted to continue living the comfortable life he had worked hard to attain.

He tucked Yuan's dream into a dark corner of his mind.

Make ready!

Grandfather continued his meditations.

51

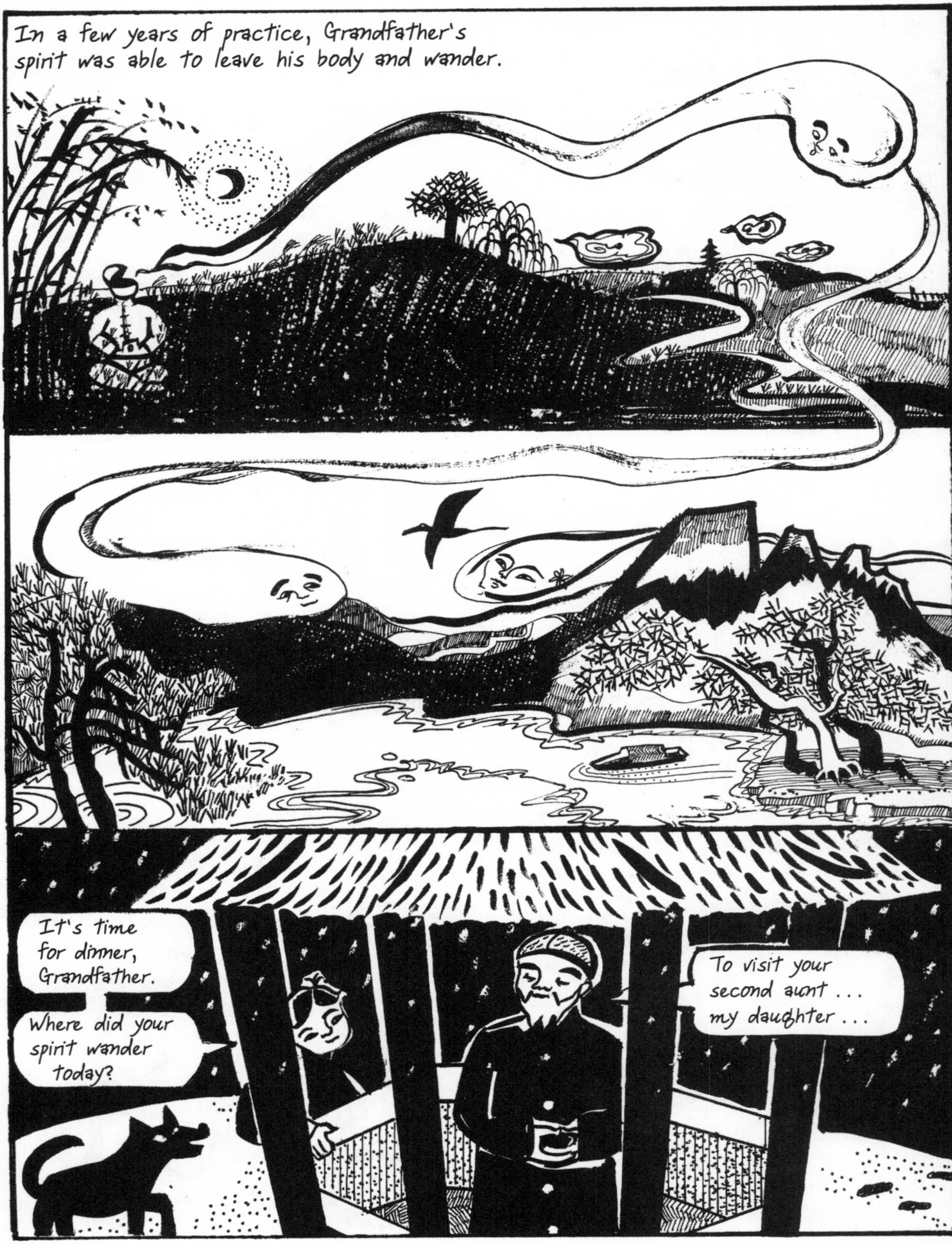
In a few years of practice, Grandfather's spirit was able to leave his body and wander.
It's time for dinner, Grandfather.
Where did your spirit wander today?
To visit your second aunt . . . my daughter . . .

What are you doing, Baba?

Planting prickly pear. Keep Rotten Egg out.

I'll put up barbed wire, too.

Don't you think cacti is enough, Baba?

The world is a dangerous place, daughter. You need to read "The Art of War" ...not to learn how to harm others but to protect yourself.

You've told me a million times—

Because you keep making mistakes.

Baba, you said something about terrible conflict, the beginning of the end—what was that about?

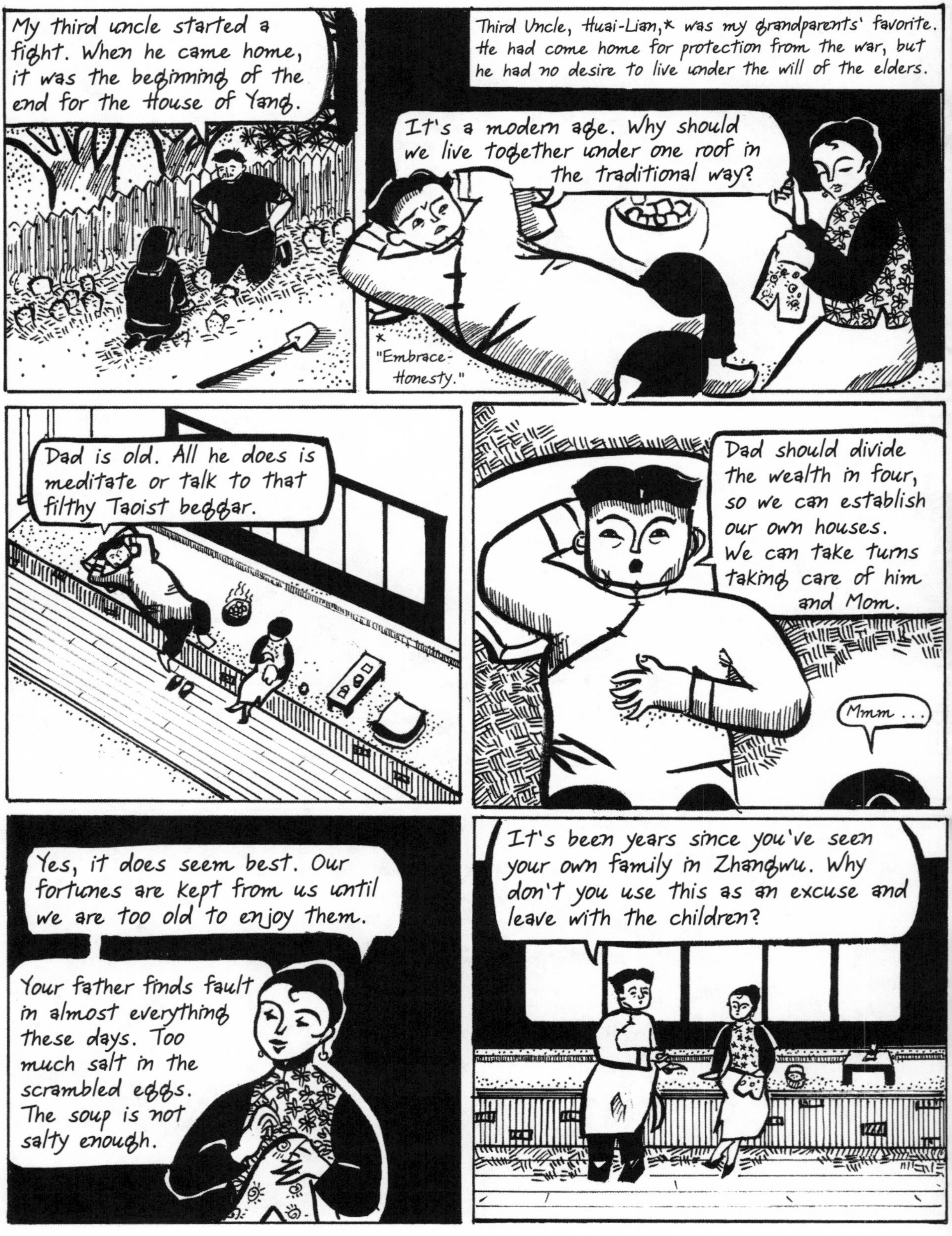
My third uncle started a fight. When he came home, it was the beginning of the end for the House of Yang.
Third Uncle, Huai-Lian,* was my grandparents' favorite. He had come home for protection from the war, but he had no desire to live under the will of the elders.
It's a modern age. Why should we live together under one roof in the traditional way?
* "Embrace-Honesty."
Dad is old. All he does is meditate or talk to that filthy Taoist beggar.
Dad should divide the wealth in four, so we can establish our own houses. We can take turns taking care of him and Mom.
Mmm . . .
Yes, it does seem best. Our fortunes are kept from us until we are too old to enjoy them.
Your father finds fault in almost everything these days. Too much salt in the scrambled eggs. The soup is not salty enough.
It's been years since you've seen your own family in Zhangwu. Why don't you use this as an excuse and leave with the children?

I have a plan on how we can extricate ourselves from this house. When I've got it all arranged, you and the kids can join me.

Meanwhile, in my parents' apartment . . .

Third Brother has been in too fine a mood. He's cheerful with everyone. I smell trouble.

My mother was stitching a pair of shoes.

For months now, Huai-Lian has been in Dad's room singing his best tunes . . . Do you know why the caged bird sings?

Because it wants to please the master?

No. It sings its prettiest, sweetest, and most enticing so you will let it out of the cage. Once it escapes, it won't ever bother to look back. It won't sing for anyone's benefit but its own.

Third Brother hasn't let on at all about his talks with Dad. He's keeping it all plugged up airtight like the inside of a gourd. Well, whatever it is, it won't be good news.

My mother was always as unflappable as a bodhisattva.

Ever since he was small, he's been sticking close to Dad and poking his nose into situations where he has no business. Dad always listens to him.

Old men have a sweet tooth for pretty words.

Dad can't abide the truth.

I was in the next room and I heard everything.

I didn't dislike my third uncle. When he came back from Linkou, he had given me a set of four books, "The Mustard Seed Manual."

I heard you're quite an artist. This should help you paint better.

Thank you, Uncle.

He gazed at me a long time. I saw that he missed Little Autumn, his son, who died of pneumonia. Little Autumn should have been my age.

He looks sad.

But Third Uncle was more often than not blind to the needs of others. His appetite was robust. He outpaced everyone at the table, unaware that others were not getting their share.

I hope he leaves some for me.

I heard that when Third Uncle was small, Master Gao, the famous scholar who taught Grandfather's four sons, had these things to say about him.

Huai-Lian is short on ambition and willpower. He'll likely spend his life eating his fill and enjoying himself without a thought of accomplishing anything . . .

Oh-ho, he's clever, but he puts his intelligence into wriggling out of work. His little arms and legs are never still. He loves to chirp fine little tunes . . .

When I scold him, he says such pretty words to me, my heart nearly melts. But as soon as my back is turned, he's at his old tricks again.

Even though Master Gao had given a bad report on my third uncle, my grandparents seemed to love him all the more for his flaws.

If you turn out to be anything at all, Dragon King up in the sky will lay two eggs in his surprise.

I'll make something of myself yet. You'll see.

Babies and small children were usually not welcome in my grandparents' apartment, but my grandparents always made an exception for Third Uncle's Little Autumn.

Grandfather was not a bit upset when Little Autumn chased Grandfather and peed on the old man's fox-lined gown.

This little grandson of mine is certainly a fearless one!

My father and his brood got a far less favorable reception.

Baba, so how did Third Uncle go about setting off on his own?

When he first returned home in the fall of 1943, he spent most of his days in Grandfather's apartment, lolling on the kang. No one else dared to be so informal.

Grandfather was giving his collection of scroll paintings an airing.

Daddy, you have huge tracts of land in the countryside and all of it under your brother's care.

Uh-huh.

Don't you see? The man has gotten fat off of you.

Hmm . . .

Every year he brings you only twenty percent of the grain harvest. That leaves him with too much profit. Why don't we go into the countryside ourselves and manage the land?

It's been decades since we've walked our own land or made a survey. Your brother allows the good land to sit fallow.

The House of Yang here in Xinmin City continues to grow, but your brother has hardly increased our yearly supply.

Daddy, I don't want to leave you. I want to stay by your side and take good care of you and Ma.

But I've been thinking the best way a good son can honor a father is to be fearless and take on the toughest jobs.

I want to help you shoulder your burdens, Daddy. I'd like to go into the countryside myself and manage the land for the benefit of us all.

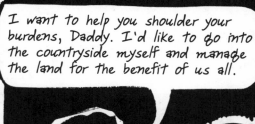

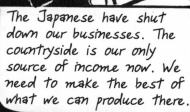

But Third Uncle wasn't looking out for anyone but himself, you see?

Well, Huai-Lian, it doesn't seem like a bad idea. I've been worrying over the matter myself.

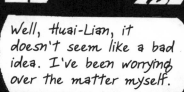

The Japanese have shut down our businesses. The countryside is our only source of income now. We need to make the best of what we can produce there.

59

Yes, we need someone honest to look to matters in the countryside.

Your brother thinks you've raised a family of idiot scholars who only know books. I'll show him scholars are just as smart at managing land.

Dad, didn't you say worries get in the way of your meditation? With me in the countryside overseeing our finances, you can concentrate.

Finally, someone is truly looking out for me.

I like it! I like your plan. But we must first discuss this with your eldest brother before we go ahead with it.

I'll have you both over tomorrow evening after dinner. I know Huai-Chao won't object, but it's only proper for us to let him in on the arrangement since he is the eldest.

My grandfather was fully confident that my father would approve.

Sigh.

Grandfather had high hopes for my father. He had given him a tough name to live up to. Huai-Chao means "Embrace-Achievements."

All Chinese parents expect too much from their kids.

This was the son Grandfather had not allowed himself to play with. There would be other sons for the spoiling.

Wah!

When Father was older, Grandfather dressed him like a little grownup and took him on his daily rounds.

Good morning, Master. Good day, Young Master.

When Father became an adult, he and Grandfather would nod stiffly to each other when they met by chance on the garden path.

Father looked like an oversized frog on his lily pad.

I didn't like Father for many reasons, but I respected him for his honesty. As far back as I can remember, my father spent most of his day in meditation.

Meditating as I do, I've never experienced a flash of understanding.

Many failed Zen practitioners would lie about attaining enlightenment.

If not meditating, he was chanting sutras in his personal shrine to Buddha. Piety and peace showed on his face . . .

. . . not the rage he showed us kids.

Children are unpaid debts from a past life.

WHAP!

WHAP!

Don't scold them at dinner. You'll give them ulcers.

You must have been a great sinner, because you have seven kids.

But Father was always gentle with my mother, who was four years his senior.

You were as dark as donkey's dung when I first laid eyes on you.

You still married me.

When mother sprained her hand, Father put up her hair for her every day.

I've heard it said that on the day of my mother's birth, the fifth day of the Fifth Moon, hailstones the size of bowls fell out of the sky.

Poor baby Yong-Qin. Hail on Dragon Boat Festival means she will have difficulties in life.

Yes, but it also means she will survive all trouble.

Yong-Qin means "Forever-Hardworking." They might as well have named her "Cow," for she worked as hard as one all her life . . .

So, as Third Uncle talked to Grandfather about taking over management of land in the countryside, Father worried.

For the life of me, I can't figure out what Huai-Lian and Dad are up to . . . Ah, it's probably nothing.

Why don't you try to meditate? It will calm you.

The next day:

Grandfather wants to see you after supper.

Ah, let's see what they will pull out of the gourd.

63

After supper Father headed for the North Garden.

Be composed . . . be calm . . . whatever they might propose.

Huai-Lian wants to go into the country and manage our land.

!

Worse than I expected! This will be utter disaster.

Our only income comes from the countryside now.

If Third Brother takes control, in time, there will be nothing for the rest of us.

For decades my brother in Shantuozi has been taking a large share of the yearly harvest.

Our household here in Xinmin has grown, but he has only increased our share a little.

I'm getting on in years. I can't go into the countryside myself.

Number Three has shown interest in managing the land. It's in our best interest to support his decision.

Huai-Chao, you're the eldest, what do you think?

What is Eldest Brother thinking?

What could my father possibly say? He knew his third brother looked only to benefit himself.

If Huai-Lian gets hold of the land, he will keep most of the harvest for himself. The rest of us will starve.

Dad, your brother in the countryside, his sons and grandsons are all farmers. Three generations of decent farmers.

How can we accuse them of taking advantage of us when every year we have had plenty to eat?

Every year they also bring us enough wood to burn. We are not in the grain business now, so what more do we need?

Dad, if we have more mouths to feed, why don't we simply ask your brother to bring us more food?

Hmm...

Tell your brother everyone has returned seeking protection here from the war. I'm sure he will do right by us.

We are an honorable family and must deal with people generously.

Also, if we demand a precise accounting of the books—as the saying goes—when the pond water is too clear, there are no fishes to be had.

66

Aside from that, if Huai-Lian goes into the countryside, he'll want to invest a great deal in livestock, equipment, silos and barns. There won't be any profit for years.

Dad, this project will only increase your financial burden when you have no other income.

I didn't expect him to have such strong arguments.

Yes, Huai-Chao, you do have a point. The Japanese have killed our businesses.

Eldest Brother is ruining my plans.

This means we will have tougher days ahead of us. From what news I can gather, the Japanese are everywhere in retreat. Rumor has it that the Americans have been smashing the Japanese fleet in the Pacific.

These are uncertain times. Inflation, corruption everywhere. Isn't it better for us to stick together, Dad?

Let's wait. In the next couple of years, the overall political situation will become clearer.

I can't wait longer. My wife and kids are waiting to join me in the countryside.

You're right. We don't know what will happen after the Japanese are gone. Let's think on this and discuss it at some point in the future.

My third uncle was as uncomfortable as an ant sitting on a hot wok. It was not proper for him to interject in what was primarily a discussion between his elders.

My father was not assured of victory. He knew Third Uncle would be whispering in Grandfather's ear again.

You're lucky you're an only child. No one to fight with.

I've always wanted an older brother to protect me.

You have to protect yourself.

Mmm...

The next morning:

Look how many of your friends dropped out of your life because Rotten Egg is stalking you.

You're too cynical, Baba.

Don't you think your father and I want our freedom too?

I wish I were free to go for a walk alone on the beach!

At your age I was already dean, overseeing thousands of students. Look at you, doing nothing.

I wanted to work or go to graduate school, but you wouldn't let me.

Rotten Egg would have found you and killed you!

...

You ruined your own life!

Ma, he's always so negative.

You have yourself to blame. When you brought Rotten Egg into our lives, your father started fighting a war again.

Sigh!

I'm sorry you've had to suffer with me.

I know it's my fault. I'm glad I have Baba's stories to write and illustrate. I'd go crazy if I didn't . . .

Was your father jealous of Third Uncle's sway over Grandfather?

No. He wanted life to remain as stable as possible in a time of turmoil.

After the conference in the North Garden, Third Uncle returned to his apartment.

He tossed and turned all night.

Eldest Brother has wrecked my plans.

How can I get back Dad's support?

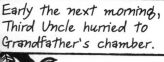

Early the next morning, Third Uncle hurried to Grandfather's chamber.

Daddy, my eldest brother says we must wait to see how everything shakes out before we can make a decision.

The days are always filled with danger.

Daddy, when the farmer sees the "lalagu," does he quit planting?

"Lalagu" is a Jerusalem cricket. They burrow and damage seedlings.

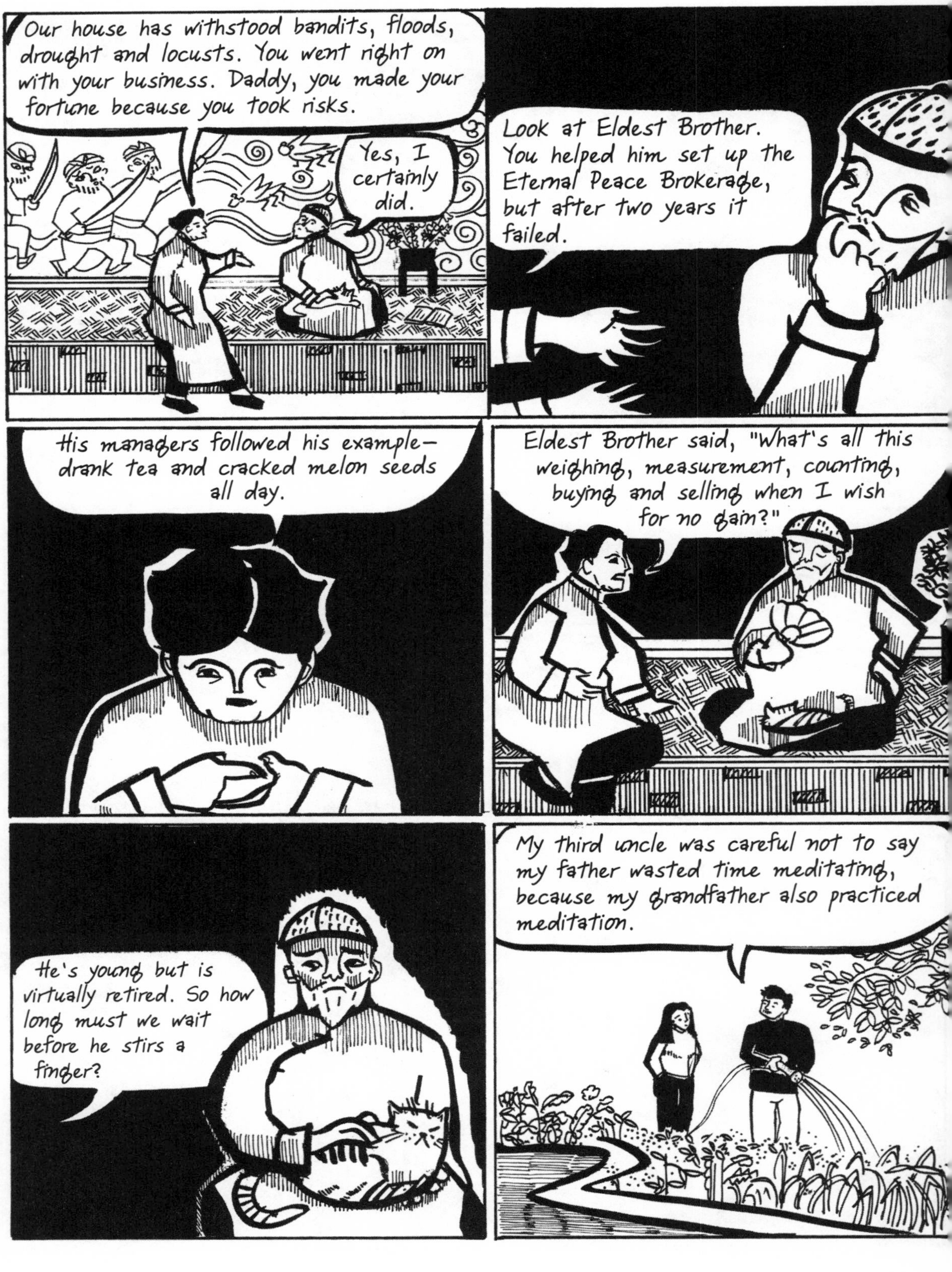
Our house has withstood bandits, floods, drought and locusts. You went right on with your business. Daddy, you made your fortune because you took risks.
Yes, I certainly did.
Look at Eldest Brother. You helped him set up the Eternal Peace Brokerage, but after two years it failed.
His managers followed his example—drank tea and cracked melon seeds all day.
Eldest Brother said, "What's all this weighing, measurement, counting, buying and selling when I wish for no gain?"
He's young but is virtually retired. So how long must we wait before he stirs a finger?
My third uncle was careful not to say my father wasted time meditating, because my grandfather also practiced meditation.

And what he said yesterday about your brother and his family being honest country folk...

don't believe it for a minute, Daddy!

Why not, Huai-Lian?

Daddy, don't I know country people best from my time in Linkou? If they manage land for you, they leave the good land to grow weeds or plant trees instead of sorghum or wheat.

The overall harvest is small, so you are fooled into thinking about selling off that supposedly unprofitable land...

or you give it away.

But once in their hands, it's all fat land.

That's how it works, Daddy.

We need to find out where our land lies, how much we have.

Eldest Brother should be doing this, but he sings the sutra all day.

You're right. We can't go on blindly. Kin is kin, blood is blood, but that doesn't mean they won't cheat us.

Daddy, you're retired but power rests firmly in your hands. You're the one to decide, not my eldest brother.

Yes, I'm certainly still the head of the house. No one can tell me what to do.

That's right, Daddy, when you asked him over, it was only out of respect for him as the eldest.

If my brother were left to himself, he'd eat an entire mountain empty of its riches.

It's time to consider my own needs . . .

I've built schools. I've fed, housed and buried the poor. I've poured money into the anti-Japanese cause.

Let's do this tomorrow night: We'll invite Huai-Chao over and tell him what we've decided.

Daddy, you'd better tell him it's all your idea.

Aiya, no problem. Your sentiments are my sentiments.

After the meeting beneath the grape arbor, my father was hardly feeling secure.

74

I heard him singing the sutra mournfully.

Emituofuo . . .

I saw him angrily weeding the spinach as the hired hands watched.

Young Master is killing more spinach than weeds.

Huai-Lian is a mischief-maker.

Educated folk say they like the farming life, but just let me trade these rags for a nice scholar's gown.

Father had not achieved the greatness Grandfather expected of an eldest son.

Everything I've tried to accomplish has come to nothing.

For Father, life was like tending a garden . . .

Every time the flowers were ready to bloom . . .

. . . nettles overtook them.

75

Buddhism teaches men to love the weeds but Father could not.

He must feel a sense of control attacking the weeds.

Third Brother is a damn nuisance.

In his twenties, he had been made the head of the provincial tax bureau with hundreds working under him.

But when the Japanese invaded Manchuria in 1931 . . .

. . . Father was forced to flee south of the Great Wall with the Young Marshal— the son of the assassinated Zhang Zuolin.

He was separated from his family for three years.

While in exile, he became the general manager of a coal mine in Tianjin. When the Young Marshal was arrested by Chiang Kai-shek, his protégés, including Father, were fired.

Chiang was the military and political leader who unified China against the warlords.

It was during this time of personal crisis that Father became a Buddhist.

I won't be coming home tonight. I'll have my vegetarian meal at the temple.

Buddhism eased his turbulent soul.

Ye-ye* tried to teach me how to circulate—"chi"—the breath of life when I stayed in Shenyang with him in 1987.

*Grandfather.

I was a dull student.

My rear is numb.

Once Father became a Buddhist, he gave away the trappings of the West.

He wore his Chinese gown and was never without his Bodhi beads. There were one hundred eight beads . . .

. . . signifying the one hundred eight afflictions and sins of mankind.

In Spring Festivals past, the gates of his Tianjin house had been bolted to keep out the stream of supplicants bearing New Year gifts.

Some bribed the gatekeeper or managed to lower gifts over the wall.

But after he lost his position, he could leave his gate wide open and not a soul would visit.

Former colleagues and friends would cross the street to avoid him.

Just like your "friends" because you are down.

He may be right.

He was saddened by the fickleness of men, but he was astonished by a sudden sense of freedom.

What do I really want?

No, not power.

Not high position.

His expression grew placid, but we kids continued to tiptoe around him . . .

His temper was still liable to erupt like a mountain of fire.

He had brought two more kids into the world, and he saw us as seven hungry mouths, gnawing on his bones.

Rancor was like a ghost pressing against the window of his soul, tapping on the panes to be let in.

His one last attempt at business was gold mining in the Miyun Mountains near Beijing.

I like it here. I get to meditate.

But the Japanese confiscated the operation in 1937 when they attacked China south of the Great Wall.

With this last failure, he took Mother and us kids home to Manchuria, seeking protection under Grandfather's roof.

He had not wanted to live in Japanese-occupied Manchuria, but the Japanese were now south of the Great Wall, so he had no reason not to go home.

Out of filial piety he gave all his savings to Grandfather's coffer; therefore, he had no money to call his own.

"Filial Piety" equals Chinese guilt complex. By American standards, we have a neurotic relationship with our parents.

I was always angry at Father when I was a kid—like when he couldn't pay my tuition—but I now understand his frustrations.

In youth, Father had raised his face heavenward with aspirations. Now his face was bent to the ground in failure.

At the first sign of blood, these poisonous insects devour the injured . . .

They are hungry enough to eat a horse or an old bull.

Baba, I understand Ye-Ye's sadness. People are afraid to contact me. And you've lost your friends, too.

After Rotten Egg shot up the office of Russell Thomson, the lawyer who befriended us, everyone seemed to drop out of touch.

My friends are advancing, and I'm just going in circles. I'm stuck.

Give me your hands.

You've got your mind and two hands. One hand for writing and the other for painting.

If your soul achieves peace, you can attain your goals.

There's that Confucian ideal again.

This peace was what my father could not achieve.

Just look at Third Brother . . .

. . . chatting with a flurry of sunflower shells, blowing out of his mouth like a winnowing machine . . . glutton.

Tea?

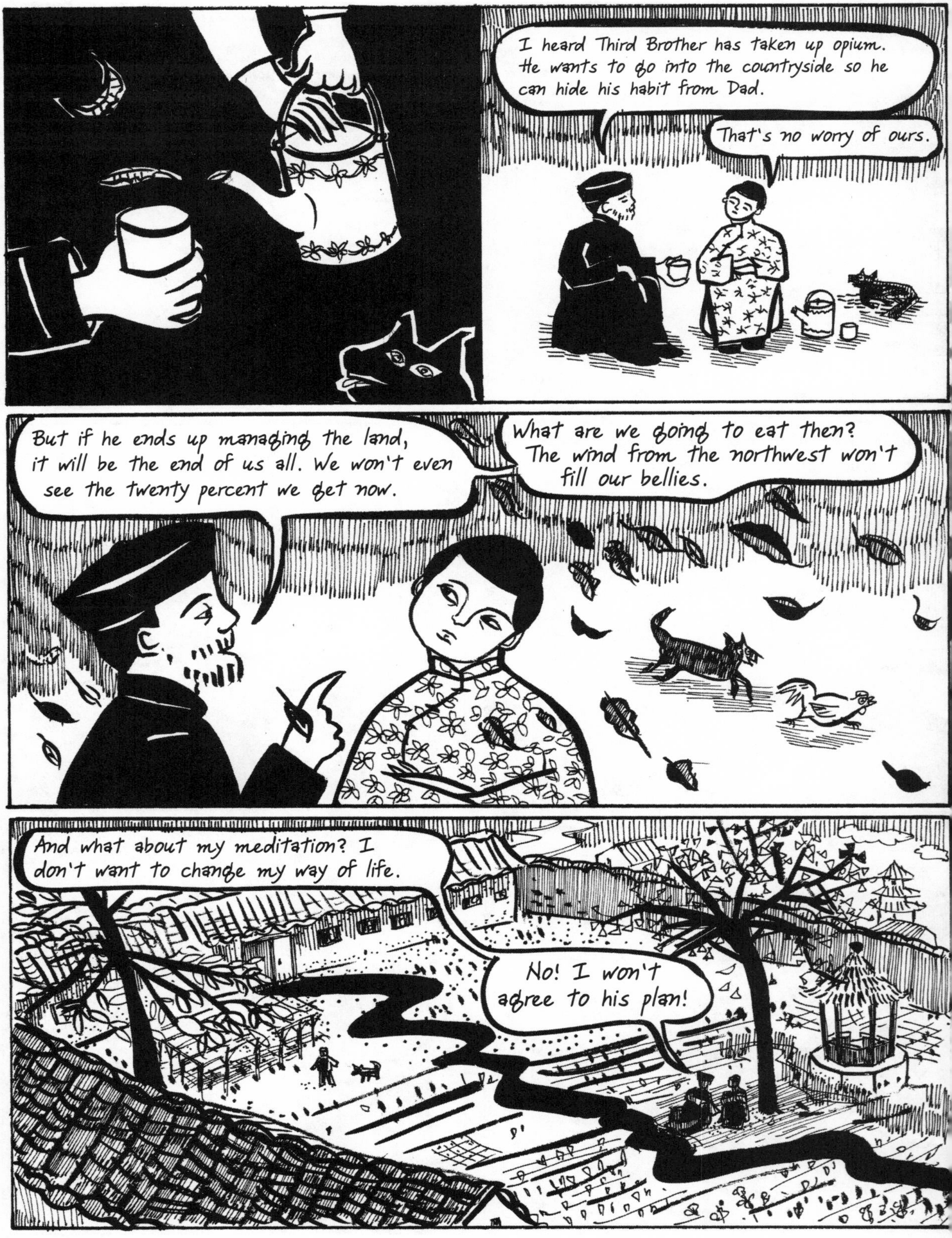
I heard Third Brother has taken up opium. He wants to go into the countryside so he can hide his habit from Dad.
That's no worry of ours.
But if he ends up managing the land, it will be the end of us all. We won't even see the twenty percent we get now.
What are we going to eat then? The wind from the northwest won't fill our bellies.
And what about my meditation? I don't want to change my way of life.
No! I won't agree to his plan!

The following evening, Father was called to the second meeting. It was impossible for him to still his pounding heart. This time he was walking into battle in full armor.

Grandfather coughed nervously.

I've decided to send Number Three into the countryside.

Hrm. Hrm.

It was the worst opening remark he could have made.

Now that everyone's home, we have too many mouths to feed.

We can't abandon our responsibility to manage our own land.

I'm too old to do it myself.

The old man spoke fast, confusing the order of his prepared remarks.

Of my four sons, Number Three has volunteered to go. Isn't this a perfect solution?

Father had anticipated these words but he still felt their shock. He would need to throw the full force of his weight against Grandfather's decision.

It was time to tear off the mask of civility.

Dad, what I say is only one person's opinion. I think we should have Second Brother and Fourth Brother join our discussion.

So you want to make it more complicated?

He called you here to talk because he respects you. As the eldest, if you nod your head, the matter will be settled.

Why are you turning this into a big issue? Why do you want the others to gang up on Dad? It's detestable. Don't forget the family fortune was made by Dad's decades of toil.

What right do you have to tell me this, Huai-Lian? Can you in all honesty tell me that you have been contributing to the family treasury?

Dad has been supplementing your income for years. When you left Zheng-jiatun, you had a mountain of debts. Dad had to bail you out!

Only then were you able to leave town.

Think of the waste.

Father spoke with the assurance of truth on his side, but to Grandfather, his words sounded like criticism against the head of the family for lack of judgment and for squandering family funds.

Sounds like one of our fights.

Tell me, Huai-Chao, you are nearly a grandfather yourself and you've not learned to say one just word.

Your life is a complete waste.

Dad, how can you be so partial to him? I am only stating the facts!

WHAM!

WHAM!

At these words, Third Uncle leapt off the kang.

If you dare to be so rude to Dad right to his face, what sort of things are you saying behind his back?

Theatrical by nature, his cries turned to sobs. In that moment the brush fire became a full conflagration.

Grandfather, on hearing his favorite son's wail of anguish, picked up his teacup . . .

. . . and threw it . . .

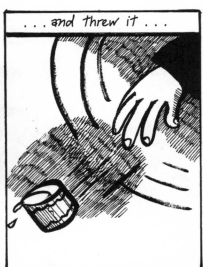

. . . at Father.

Grandfather picked up the ink slab, the brushes and the brush rest and flung them.

And for a grand finale . . .

You have done too much evil, Third Brother! You have done much evil!

I warn you. Be careful for the bombs are falling like sheets of rain. It is a time of grave danger, and you must act in good conscience, my brother, lest one of them falls on your head.

Father pushed past the astonished eavesdroppers.

Ingrate!

I felt terrible for Father.

There is nothing worse than being unjustly accused.

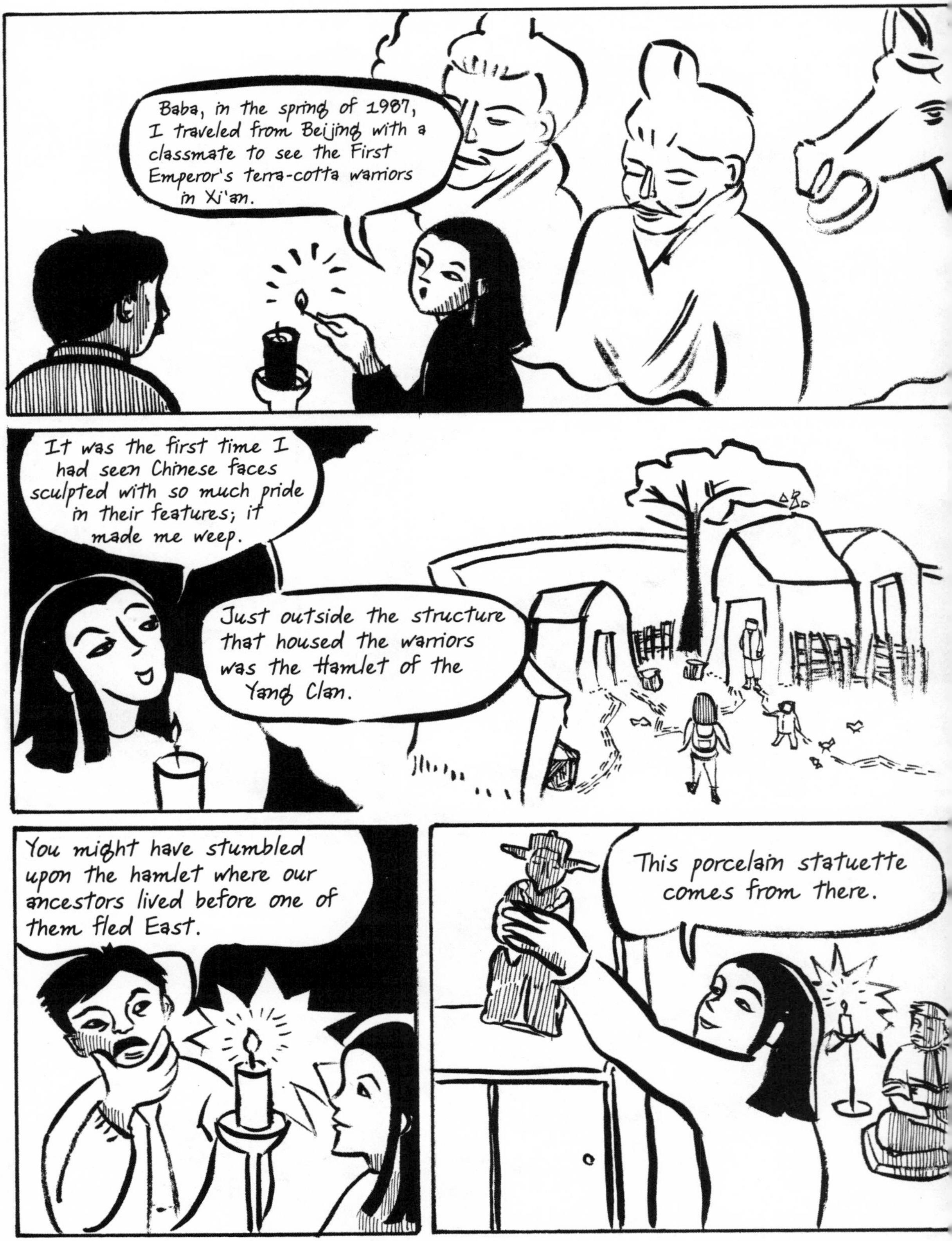
Baba, in the spring of 1987, I traveled from Beijing with a classmate to see the First Emperor's terra-cotta warriors in Xi'an.
It was the first time I had seen Chinese faces sculpted with so much pride in their features; it made me weep.
Just outside the structure that housed the warriors was the Hamlet of the Yang Clan.
You might have stumbled upon the hamlet where our ancestors lived before one of them fled East.
This porcelain statuette comes from there.

He's certainly handsome. Most likely from the Ming Dynasty, because the glaze is darker than the Qing blue.

I just saw something very much like him at a museum.

Here is something I've never shown you.

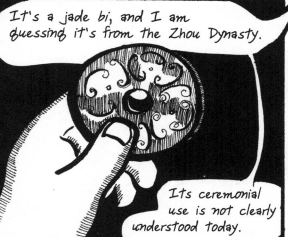

It's a jade bi, and I am guessing it's from the Zhou Dynasty.

Its ceremonial use is not clearly understood today.

Jade represents the highest ideals of men, like purity and fortitude.

Oooh, it has an inner glow.

And so cool and smooth.

Baba, can I wear this on a cord?

Certainly not.

When you fled Rotten Egg, you lost everything, including the antique jade pieces Mama gave you.

You even lost your car.

How do you expect me to trust you with anything?

I'm sorry, Baba. I made a lot of bad choices.

Well, I promised to continue . . .

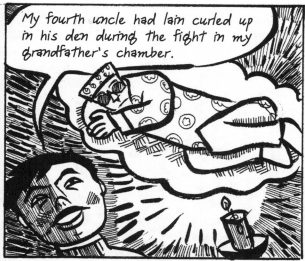

My fourth uncle had lain curled up in his den during the fight in my grandfather's chamber.

Like my father, Fourth Uncle did not want Third Uncle to take over the land in the countryside. It did not take a prophet to predict the difficulties in store for the House of Yang in Xinmin if this were to happen.

But Fourth Uncle let Father bear the blows alone.

He rarely crooked a little finger to aid another, unless he was certain it would not cost him anything.

Master Gao had very little to say about Grandfather's youngest son.

This child always does his lessons without fuss but without any flair either. He tags along quietly after his brothers.

Fourth Uncle grew to be the tallest of the brothers, but he stooped.

Was it because he wanted to make himself as unobtrusive as possible?

Maybe.

Grandfather named him Huai-Zheng, which means "Embrace-Integrity." He was always nicely groomed, his hair anointed with fragrant oil.

I could never get a good look at his eyes behind the tinted "tea" glasses.

If my cousins and I ran into him along the garden path, we would scoot politely to the side to let him pass.

If we found him walking behind us, we churned our legs faster to increase the distance as if avoiding Yama, the Judge of Hell.

His brothers had seniority over him in every aspect of life, so he took out his frustrations on us kids.

If we ruined his afternoon nap with our noise, he ordered us to stand in circles he marked in the dirt.

We stood for hours in the summer heat . . .

. . . until we were ready to keel over . . .

My Second Aunt—the one who died before the forsythias could bloom—pleaded our case before Grandmother and came to our rescue.

You may go, you rascals.

While his brothers were allowed to leave when opportunities in other cities beckoned, Fourth Uncle was made to remain at Grandfather's side and scrupulously disciplined.

One son was needed at home to watch over the elders.

Surprised by his father's appearance . . .

. . . Fourth Uncle tucked the hand that held the cigarette into his sleeve.

Ahem . . . what have you got there, Huai-Zheng?

He stamped out his cigarette

Family members always knew when Fourth Uncle was paid his monthly salary, for on that day, he invariably brought home a piece of pork tied to one end of a string as a gift to his parents.

Why is he walking funny?

He doesn't want grease on his gown.

Kissing up again...

His wife boasted no culinary gift, yet she and Fourth Uncle insisted she cook the meat for the elders.

The old people had much finer food to eat, but the gesture was a show of filial piety.

It's a lot of extra work for you, my girl.

Oh, it's no trouble at all. It is my good fortune that my worthless dish will warm your stomachs. Father, I am happiest when I am able to serve you.

You've given shelter to my old dad, my brother and his wife. I can't possibly repay you in this lifetime and the next.

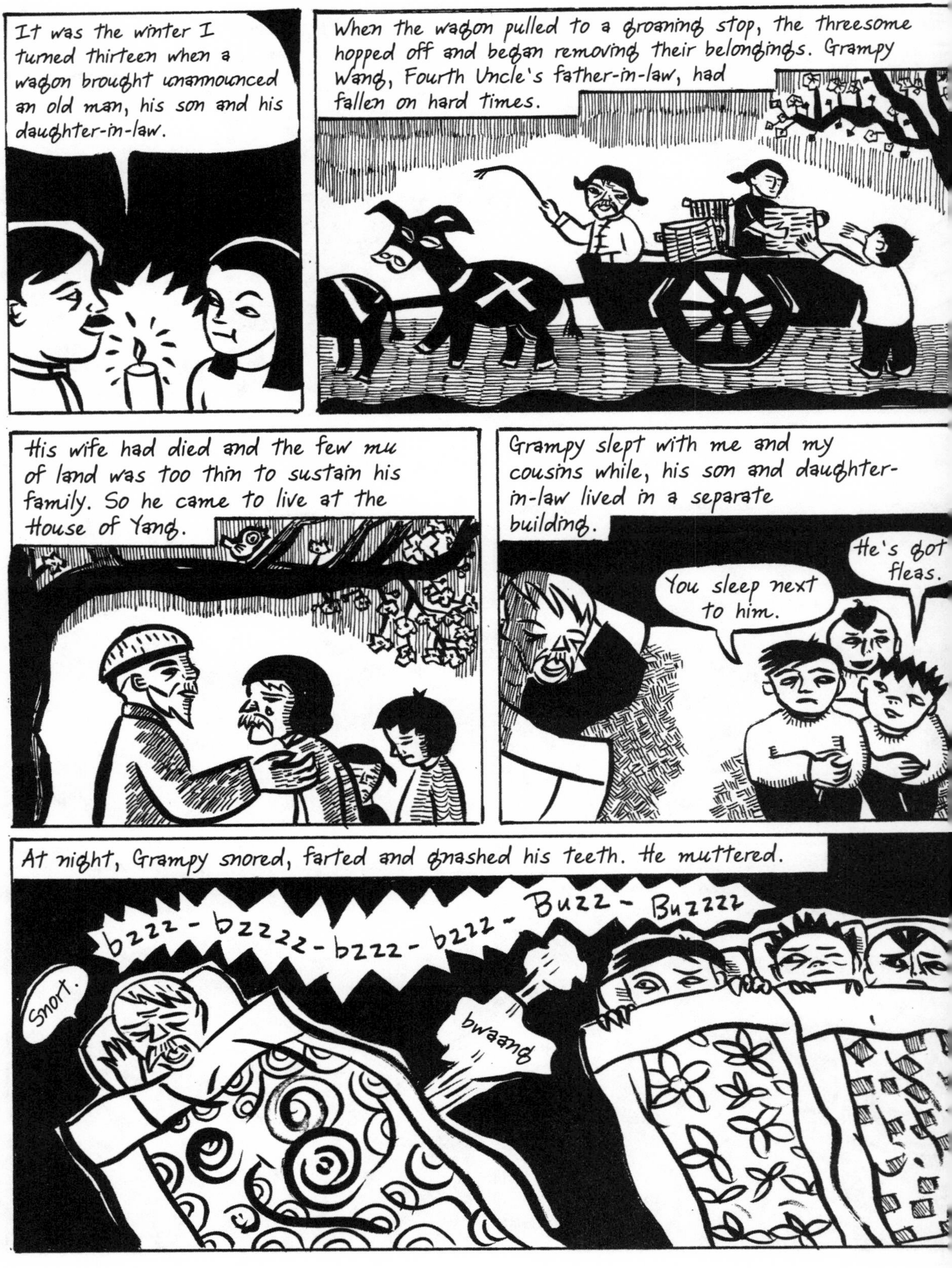
It was the winter I turned thirteen when a wagon brought unannounced an old man, his son and his daughter-in-law.
When the wagon pulled to a groaning stop, the threesome hopped off and began removing their belongings. Grampy Wang, Fourth Uncle's father-in-law, had fallen on hard times.
His wife had died and the few mu of land was too thin to sustain his family. So he came to live at the House of Yang.
Grampy slept with me and my cousins while, his son and daughter-in-law lived in a separate building.
You sleep next to him.
He's got fleas.
At night, Grampy snored, farted and gnashed his teeth. He muttered.
bzzz-bzzzz-bzzz-bzzz-Buzz-Buzzzz
Snort.
bwaang

He spat and missed the spittoon.

He screamed in the night.

He searched our bedding.

Grandfather found Grampy's son a position as an apprentice to a tailor, and after three years, the young man was finally able to make his own home and invited Grampy to live with him and his wife.

Fourth Uncle's Wife should indeed have been grateful to Grandfather.

Aside from Grandfather and Grandmother, the only other member of the household to whom Fourth Uncle showed a degree of warmth was his youngest sister.

Do you like it?

I always wanted a watch.

Most adults can't afford a watch.

She was Grandfather and Grandmother's last child. They lavished their love on her. I addressed her as Youngest Aunt, but she was only a year older than me.

How funny to have auntie for a playmate.

Grandfather gave her a little red tricycle, at which I could only stare with envy.

Grandfather never let her go to bed upset, lest she had nightmares.

98

Fourth Uncle knew it pleased Grandfather to see him look after Youngest Aunt, so he went about it with great showmanship.

Fourth Uncle was a talented musician. He could play songs like *Swallow Flying in Pairs*. The music wafted into the garden on summer evenings.

He had an expensive Double-Phoenix brand organ and he spent long hours teaching Young Aunt.

She's no better than she was a year ago.

He had a good reason for lavishing lessons on her.

Who was visiting Ma and Dad today?

What did they talk about?

What gifts did they bring?

She did not know it, but she was his little informer.

Oh, Mr. and Mrs. Liu came and they brought mung bean cakes—I hate those—they talked about boring things like the Japanese and the cost of grain.

Fourth Uncle had become interested in the radio as soon as it came along in the latter days of the Japanese occupation.

Thousands of American and British casualties, but the Japanese Imperial Army has met with little loss of men.

These were lies we heard on Manchukuo news.

Censorship of news grew even tighter as the Japanese began losing battles in the Pacific. Only with highly placed connections, and a good deal of money and government approval, was he able to get a radio.

Fourth Uncle raised poles and strung wires between them to receive news from the faraway wartime capital of Chongqing, where Chiang Kai-shek's Nationalist government had retreated in 1938 from the Japanese.

← antenna

Let's listen in at two a.m. We have to be careful no one knows.

Nationalist news reports came only in the early morning hours and the reception was weak.

Fourth Uncle also installed a speaker in Grandfather's room.

Dad, tell me what you like. When the program is available, I'll turn the radio on.

These newfangled things are magic.

He liked dagu, the comic dialogues, stories sung by women, accompanied by the tapping of a drum, which he heard in his youth.

The installation of the speaker seemed the act of a good son, but the speaker encased a microphone, so Fourth Uncle could eavesdrop on the elders from his own apartment.

I walked in on Fourth Uncle on an errand one day when I tried to deliver a message to him.

How peculiar! I hear Grandfather and his guests!

I pretended I had not noticed anything out of the ordinary, so I delivered the message and left.

My father asked me to tell you . . .

Soon after, Fourth Uncle installed an electric buzzer on the door.

BUZZ

Oh, the alarm is just for the fun of it.

How can it be for fun? It makes everyone leap a foot off the ground!

I knew he needed the alarm to warn him when he was listening in on the elders.

Well, it's also protection against burglars.

But a thief would have to go through a garden gate and two sets of doors to steal anything.

Secretive Fourth Uncle did not need to step foot outside his room to tune in to the fight in Grandfather's chamber. The shattering of the teapot on the floorboards came in loud and clear through the hidden microphone.

Your life is a complete waste.

Dad, how can you be so partial to him?

CRASH

Even if Dad himself comes looking for me, I'm not going to take sides.

Good idea.

I'm feeling pretty good, but I'll use my health as an excuse—cough loudly a few times and they will leave me alone.

COUGH COUGH COUGH COUGH COUGH COUGH

Earlier that year in 1943, Fourth Uncle had come down with tuberculosis. Grandfather suggested he quit his job.

Huai-Zheng, there is blood on your handkerchief.

He did so without further encouragement. The Matriarch funded his expensive taste for musical instruments, radios and other newfangled Western things.

There was no cure for TB in those days. It was said that eating spinach was an effective remedy, so in the North Garden half a *mu* of spinach was planted.

Stir-fried, boiled, stewed, Fourth Uncle ate spinach in every way imaginable.

Fourth Uncle was up early and circling the big South Garden for exercise. It was the first time I saw him step foot into the garden, for he disdained anything that had to do with farm labor.

Even in heavy snow, he did not miss his daily exercise. He went about curing himself as methodically and diligently as he did fixing a broken clock or radio.

Enjoying your walk, sir?

His long eyebrows were frosted white.

His heart must be frosted over, too.

As much as I disliked Fourth Uncle, I loved my second uncle. He was the joker in the family.

SCRATCH

I never quibble over minutiae, but go after the big prize. If I succeed, I'll be like Liu Bang, the founder of the Han.

Hey, but if I fail, I'll follow the Art of War: Of the thirty-six strategies, the superior policy is to run away.

HA HA HA HA HA HA HA

When he came home from Shenyang, he took one of the remote northern units along Market Street.

This was the wish of his cross-eyed wife, who did not want to be irritated on a daily basis by the beauty and wealth of Third Uncle's wife.

In his remote kingdom of the North Garden, Second Uncle did not lack for gossip.

Elder Brother and Third Brother didn't show up for breakfast . . . still feuding.

104

Second Uncle went about his daily business. He laughed and joked as if he had heard nothing.

Grandfather had named his second son Huai-Zhi, meaning "Embrace-Determination."

This son of yours, if he should succeed in life, his achievements will be too big to measure.

On the other hand, if he goes bad, he is likely to go very, very bad. He fools around all day long...

...but he's the smartest of your bunch. He's got the keenest memory, knows just what's important in his studies and ignores the rest.

Keep an eye on that boy, because he has a taste for the dangerous. Keep a rein on him and gently steer him toward success.

But what Master Gao did not tell Grandfather was how to discipline Second Uncle.

How do we keep him on the proper path?

Yes, if we are too strict with Second Son, we might stultify the spirit of genius.

My grandparents indulged his genius and continued to do so when he grew into a man. He was the only son allowed to smoke . . .

His coat was pitted with burn marks from cigarette ash.

Second Uncle was by nature a Taoist. Taoists believe that it is man and his activities that afflict an otherwise perfect world.

Why don't you look after your kids and educate them properly?

Children are in a state of perfection and cannot be improved. Take, for example, a sphere. You go at it with a piece of sandpaper, hoping to make it even more spherical . . .

. . . and you've done damage. It becomes less than spherical. Kids are all born spheres. They don't need my tampering.

Take the tortoise. You think, what a clumsily made animal. So slow. A frog with one leap goes a great long way.

But Granddaddy Heaven destined each to have his own way to negotiate the world.

Feel sorry for the tortoise and take his shell away? He won't survive. Feel sorry for the frog, fleshy and exposed? Clamp a shell on him, he'll develop fungus.

My kids will make their way through the world in their own fashion, at their own level of comfort.

During Spring Festival, he did not disdain to join the women at cards.

Those were very poor moves. I know your hands. I have a troop of little men at my command who can peer over your shoulders.

Show them to us.

Oh-ho, that won't be necessary. No matter how hard you look, they won't be visible to your eyes.

When Second Uncle began attending boarding school in Shenyang, he was good in all subjects, but he was especially good with numbers.

Soon after graduation, he disappeared. Grandfather searched nearly a year for him and thought him dead. It was 1925, during the second war between Zhang Zuolin and rival warlord Wu Peifu for control of Beijing.

Second Uncle returned in late fall, when Zhang returned victorious after putting down the mutiny of Guo Songlin.

I loved to listen to his stories. He was circumspect about his own involvement in the mutiny of Guo, known as Devil Guo for his training in Japan, the land of the "Small Devils."

He should have crossed the river Liao immediately—surprised Warlord Zhang—instead of trying to assemble his men in fancy military formations.

Devil Guo was no man of action. His soldiers were the prettiest. None with moles and pockmarks, none too short or too tall, wearing the most handsome uniforms.

He should have fought straight into Shenyang and given them a big ol' boo! Then he would have become Supreme Commander himself.

And when Thick-Tongued Wu—so named for his stutter—came riding across the ice with his warriors like a pack of crows, he should have put on rabbit shoes and hopped on out of there.

To keep alive is the only strategy. Death is death. Failure isn't running away, my friends. Failure is dying. He failed because he let himself get killed.

Guo and his wife were dragged out from a hole in the ground where peasants store cabbages—

and Bang! Bang! Just like that, they lay dead in the snow like a couple of fishes.

Old Granddaddy Heaven allotted each man his share of the thing called life. If he dies in war or perishes in fire or flood, it's obvious his portion is all used up.

But how he lives his allotted days is entirely up to him.

He had to have been there to tell these stories with so much heat.

Second Uncle said that if the length of men's lives were determined by Granddaddy Heaven, there was no reason why men should fuss and haggle over trifles.

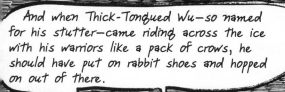

I love his worldview.

You met his son—my cousin—Little Aizi.

Bring me your China photo album.

He was a snot-nosed kid. We fought a lot and he'd tattle to his mother about me.

He was visiting Grandmother and Ye-ye in Shenyang on New Year's Day after a morning of fishing.

Second Uncle did not educate his kids. He knew the Communists were coming, and those who thought little beyond fishing would be the ones to survive in the new order.

So after Grandfather had thrown the teapot . . .

...Father, blinded by anger and a sense of injustice, staggered back to his quarters.

He settled down on his cushion without a word and remained motionless.

At last, he said:

That brat, Number Three, is making a mess of things.

Mother sat in silence, thinking hard on the recent events and occasionally taking a hard look at Father.

Best to keep quiet— I don't want to make matters worse.

In the tense days that followed the fight, Father recited the Buddhist scriptures. The qing rang out mournfully. He stopped only for naps and meals, which were brought to him to be eaten alone.

He was up at cockcrow to meditate.

Grandfather also tried to meditate, but his belly was still puffed to bursting with anger. He spoke very little to anyone.

Father and son—one living in the eastern extreme of the long row of apartments, the other in the western extreme—were as silent as feuding monks from rival monasteries.

On the surface, Third Uncle, Huai-Lian, had won, but in reality his future remained undecided. There were no strains of opera drifting from his apartment . . .

I can't go ahead with my plans until those two come to terms.

. . . only the measured sound of his footsteps back and forth, back and forth across the floorboards, as his thoughts paced between hope and frustration.

My wife and kids are anxious to join me in the countryside.

In the morning, Third Uncle made his way up the length of the North Garden. The stumps of the harvested cabbages were damp with dew.

The only person who can mediate is Second Brother.

Second Uncle had anticipated his visit and knew what the man was coming for.

The magic paper men in his pocket told him, right, Baba?

MREOW!

To what do we owe the pleasure of your company?

Third Uncle pretended not to hear the tone of mockery.

Second Uncle spoke about everything except what Third Uncle was burning to address.

Well, this is fine weather for the harvest.

My gout is acting up again.

My youngest has a cold.

...

He's fidgeting as if he's sitting on boils.

Ha, ha, ha, so Mr. Wang said to me . . .

You want to hear my new poem?

When he could no longer contain himself, he spilled his thoughts like beans from a pouch.

No. No, Second Brother, I wish to manage the land.

Eldest and Dad had a big fight. Dad's on my side and he threw the teapot at Eldest, so now they're not talking . . .

Ha, ha. Well it certainly looks like you've done a good job of offending Eldest. Now you come to me for help.

Eldest Brother will just blow up in my face if I go talk to him. The best thing to do is to stash it, sleep on it and see how it all looks in a month or so.

I can't afford to waste another minute.

Stash it?

Sleep on it?

Brother, you've got to go and speak to him on my behalf.

Only you have the power to sway him. Please!

I have always held you in the highest esteem.

People trust your judgment.

You can patch things up between Eldest and me.

Please, go talk to Eldest, will you?

Yes, go tomorrow.

The longer you wait, the worse it will be.

Yes, go tomorrow.

Tomorrow will be best.

Second Uncle liked prolonging his brother's torment.

Well . . . if you think it is wise. But, like I said, everyone's belly is bloated with anger.

I can't guarantee results.

Oh, all right, I will go tomorrow and sound out Eldest.

Get some sleep, you look positively dreadful.

114

Next morning, Second Uncle went to see Grandfather.

As usual, Second Uncle was full of jokes and anecdotes to coax a smile from Grandfather.

...and that's why three thirsty monks will carry less water in a bucket than one thirsty monk.

After the jokes, he was ready to broach the subject.

When a son argues with his father, no matter what the reason for the disagreement, it is always the son's fault.

Children must not be disrespectful.

It is my brother's fault, no matter how you look at it.

Hrrm, hrrm. I think it is rightly so.

It is indisputably so. I will go talk to my elder brother. I will tell him it is time for him to apologize.

What do you think, Dad?

Grandfather had no reason to object. Here was someone offering to mediate.

That Fourth Son is useless as a peace maker. He can't be pried out of his stronghold with its annoying buzzer.

Yes, but do not say I sent you.

Here is an opportunity for everyone to back down without losing face.

I won't approach Eldest until tomorrow. Let Number Three stew for another day.

It was four days after the big fight when Second Uncle went to see father. The edge of Father's anger had been blunted. He, too, was hoping to repair the relationship.

Now my family welfare rests entirely in Dad's hands. I need to make peace with him.

Father and Second Uncle had always been close. They were only two years apart.

Sooo, my sister-in-law, have you noticed my wife's getting more cross-eyed?

Why, yes, it does seem so.

Seem so? Why, of course, it is so.

Then isn't it time you took her to see a doctor?

Mother suddenly realized he'd been pulling her leg.

Well, why should she look at you out of the corners of her eyes?

Ah, but don't you know, every day she looks at me out of the corners of her eyes in disgust. That's the reason she grows more cross-eyed by the day.

HA HA

Because I'm getting old and useless and she likes the sight of me less.

Ha, ha, ha. Number Two, one can never get a serious word out of you.

Eldest Brother, I know you very well. You are just like Chen Ping of history.

When Chen Ping was a young man, he was appointed to divide up a pig among his fellow villagers.

If you think I'm fair with the meat now...

...when I become prime minister one day, I will be just as fair-minded.

Well, it was destiny, for he did become the prime minister to the first emperor of the Han Dynasty.

I'm far from the talent of Chen Ping, but I am fair and just.

You know as well as I do, if Huai-Lian takes over management of the land, we'll soon be begging food in bowls made of gold.

Sure, we have land and property to our name, but what good will those do us when our bellies are empty?

But look, Brother, if you were to go against Dad, it will be like the arm wrestling with the leg. You can't win.

It's okay for you to struggle with Huai-Lian, but don't fight Dad. You've got the wrong guy.

Besides, Dad hasn't been feeling strong lately. You know, he's over seventy.

Second Uncle knew just how to instill guilt in Father's heart.

Now Huai-Lian wants to manage the land. Don't set yourself against him.

You're talking for the rest of us, but arguing with Dad won't prevent it.

Don't waste your energy playing the hero to save the situation, because you simply don't have the power to do so. Let them do what they will.

The best thing for you now is to take all your children over to see Dad and apologize. There is no shame in expressing it.

Remember, Elder Brother, you are Buddha's disciple. Buddha must reign in your heart, not demons.

A Buddhist must empty himself. Don't fill yourself up with anger. This is Buddha's path.

If you don't apologize, your days will be painful, and your heart will always be in turmoil. How can you possibly meditate? The bitter sea is limitless.

But turn yourself around, and you will soon find yourself securely on land again. To attain enlightenment, you must empty yourself.

Yes, Second Brother is absolutely right. You should go over and apologize to remove this sword that hangs over all of us. It's time you learned to say a few honeyed words.

You expect the world to know you're true, decent and honest without advertisement. Don't you know old people are just like kids? They like sweets.

Number Three has been chirping sweetly to Dad since he was a baby.

With Mother's nudging, Father agreed to make the apology.

I will apologize tomorrow night but only if Number Three is not there. I want to make it clear, I am not apologizing to Huai-Lian!

No problem. I've thought it all through. Trust me. I will arrange it to your satisfaction.

Next evening:

Storm clouds bore down rapidly from the northwest. Reeds in the North Garden trembled and clattered. There was no bird song except for a thrush's solo at the end of the day.

Everyone was eager to end the family strife, but no one could be certain it would result in a satisfying end.

Let's go over to see Grandfather.

My eldest and second brothers were already married: one had moved away and the other refused to take part in the apology.

After dinner, after the bowls, dishes, pots and pans had been put away, a great quiet settled over the house like snowfall, as if everyone was holding his breath.

Number Three is not in the room.

SIGH

Dad is waiting.

I've never performed this kind of somber act before. I'm worried. I hope it all turns out well.

Grandfather did not look up. He was pretending he had not been anxiously awaiting the interview.

Cushion for Father to kneel more comfortably.

Dad, I've been thinking hard. I was wrong to go against you. I was taken by stupidity.

My words were disrespectful. It is wrong for a son to act the way I did. I'm here to ask for your forgiveness.

It's painful to see a man his age kneel at someone's feet to declare himself guilty when in fact he is not.

Grandfather looked at us kids expectantly. I knew it was time for us to make our kowtow.

The three younger ones behind me did not understand the gravity of the situation. They giggled as they prostrated.

How many? I better make two just to be on the safe side.

Dad, look how respectful and obedient are your son and grandchildren.

You may sit down. Children, enough. No more kowtows.

Go on. Go out and play.

The younger ones wondered why the fun had ended.

After we kids left, the men began to talk in earnest.

Father, if you wish Number Three to go manage our land, then he should do so.

As the saying goes, "While there is water, we must make the clay."

Grandfather was happy to hear Father give his consent.

After we had left Grandfather's room, we returned to keep Mother company. I waited to listen to the result of the meeting.

Father's color had ebbed when he entered. He climbed on the *kang*, lifting the skirts of his gown before coming to rest on his reed cushion.

TAP TAP TAP

Lingzi, hurry and get your father a towel.

If I had known that it would all come to this, we should have stayed south of the Great Wall.

We could have managed somehow. Now our fate is entirely in the hands of others.

I've never heard Mother give in to sadness.

In my past life, I must have done too many bad things. I owe too much for my sins.

He cast accusatory glances at us children, as if we were the embodiment of his errors.

I wanted to shout, "We had to follow after you to do the dirty work when we were completely guiltless."

Mother rescued us from his tirade.

Kids, why don't you go outside?

Let's get out of here.

The fight had come to an end, but there was no real peace. The mood had changed irrevocably.

Not long ago, when far-flung family members had come together to find protection from the war under Grandfather's roof, the house had become lively.

Now family life tasted dull like a dish in which the cook had forgotten to add the salt.

Prrrr

The men no longer supped together. Third Uncle ate with the Patriarch. Fourth Uncle was on his strict diet of spinach for his health, which his wife cooked for him in the privacy of their own apartment. Second Uncle and Father ate like hermits.

The sisters-in-law were awkward with one another, as were the older children. They ate with bowed heads in near silence and went about their own business as soon as they were done.

In the immediate days after the fight, Third Uncle and Grandfather drew up plans for the move to the countryside.

I need funds to buy equipment, horses, cows, sheep and goats, to build a house and granaries, sheds . . .

Autumn of 1944 arrived. I was sixteen and in my last month of high school. Classes were held infrequently, and when they convened, most of the hours were spent at air-raid drills. One Saturday afternoon, I returned home from school to find Third Uncle busy in the yard, loading the wagon.

No family had come out to lend him a hand. Only the new wagoner assisted him in loading the heavier objects. Since the fight, everyone had been cool toward him.

They watched his activities through the windows.

The following morning, after Third Uncle had eaten breakfast with Grandfather, he harnessed two horses and a mule to the wagon. A third horse was hitched to the back.

Now that the family's hope for the future lay in the countryside, the center of power was shifting from Xinmin to ancestral Shantuozi.

No one has come out to say good-bye except me.

Once the wagon had disappeared from view, I walked through the big South Gate. It was Sunday morning, and few people were about. I felt a strange smoky, sour emptiness inside my chest.

After my walk, I felt no better. I walked into the barn.

With the four draft animals gone, only the donkey remained. The three horses and the mule had always bullied the smaller beast—they would nudge him out of the way when feeding.

The trough had been designed for horses, which was on the tall side for the short-legged donkey.

Now you have it quite nice, don't you, little one? No one to bother you.

The donkey shook its ears and looked at me with his soulful eyes.

But you've got your work cut out for you. You must mill the grain alone.

Everything seems so desolate. With Third Uncle going into the countryside, it should feel like a new beginning. Instead, it feels like the end of a banquet.

Is this how it is to have brothers? Each one of us will grow up and go his own way?

I couldn't get rid of an awful sensation in my chest. I remembered what Idiot Yuan had told my grandfather a year before.

Yang Junchen, beware!

The old ways will disappear. There will be chaos. Relationships will be perverted. Heaven and earth will be turned upside down. Rulers will be killed. Sons will betray fathers.

130

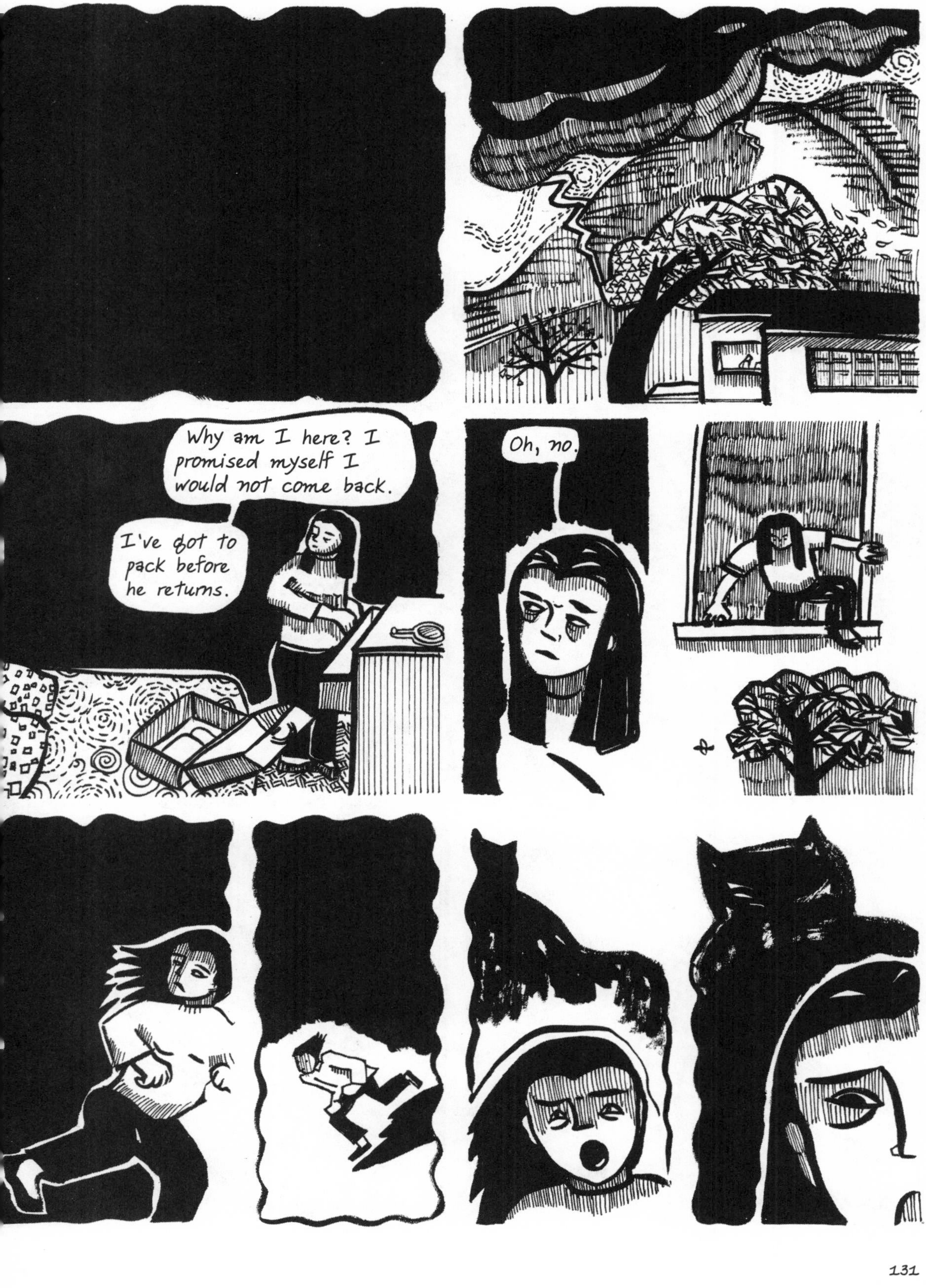
Why am I here? I promised myself I would not come back.
I've got to pack before he returns.
Oh, no.

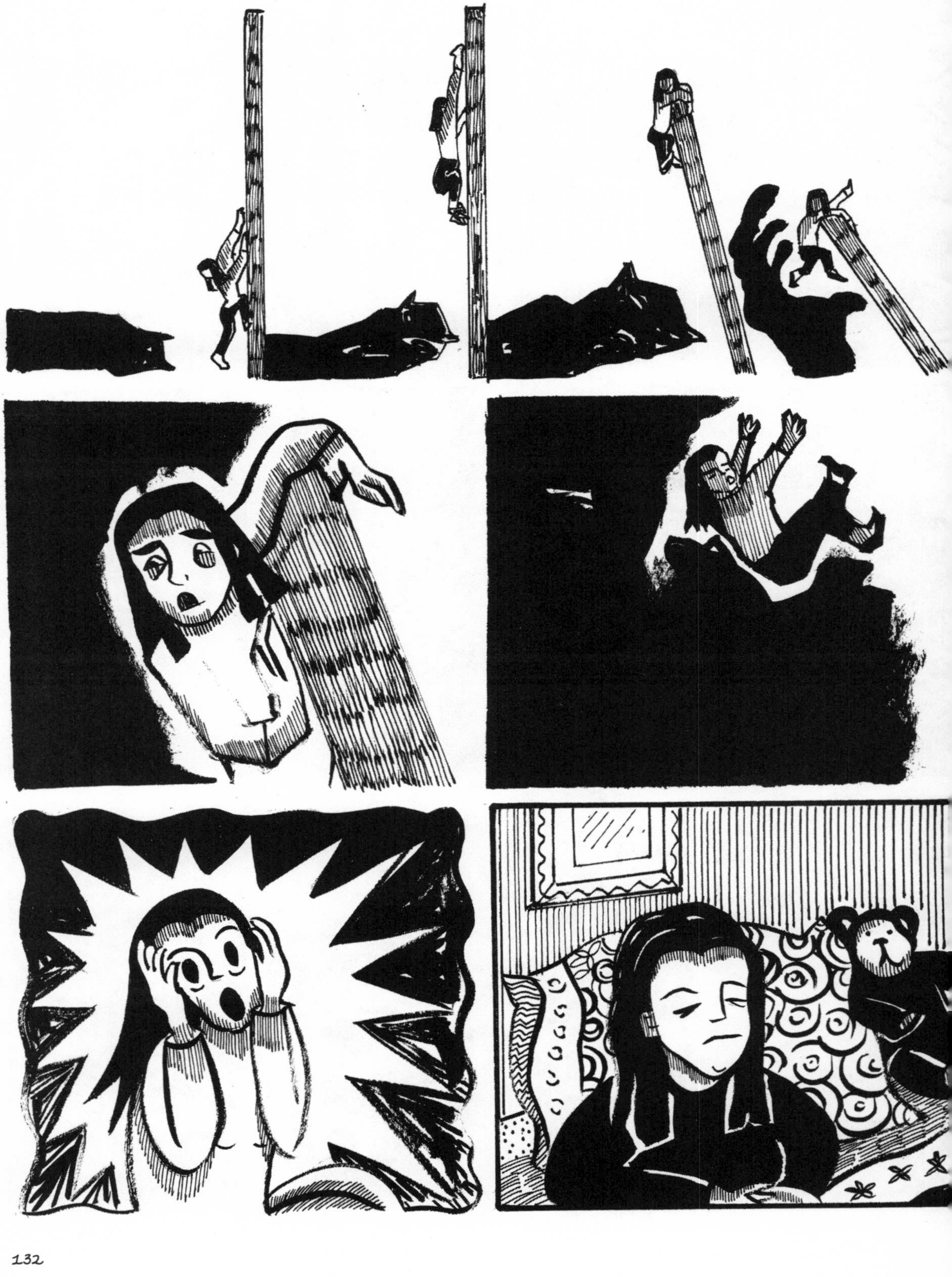

Baba, I had a bad dream again. This time, I was climbing a wall to get away, only the wall toppled and I fell right back into Rotten Egg's grasp.

Your wounds were too deep. The nightmares may never stop. We'll go for a walk after breakfast and get out from under this gloom.

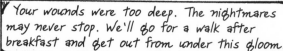

Baba, there's that Chinese saying, "You need to fight with a man to know a man..."

I've fought with you plenty, so I guess I am getting to know you better.

Thank heaven, now your fights go only hours, not days.

Did your father and grandfather get to know each other better after the fight?

Everyone came back to the family home in the fall of 1943. To Grandfather, the traditional bimonthly family council seemed all the more necessary.

The council embodied his authority over the House of Yang. But the peace that reigned after the fight was tense, as if one word out of anyone would bring the shaky structure of the house down on all of our heads.

134

After Third Uncle's departure, Mother's new daughter-in-law stood by her side.

Yong-Qin, your hair . . .

do you have flour caked in it?

No, Dad. I didn't cook tonight.

My head is turning gray.

I've been blind to her needs. She has been attending to me faithfully since she was a young bride.

Don't trouble yourself to come to the family councils, Yong-Qin. You deserve the respect that comes with age.

Grandfather then turned his attention to Second Uncle's cross-eyed wife. She, unlike Third Uncle's pretty spouse, came from a family whose fortune was in decline.

The match had been made soon after Second Uncle reappeared at the House of Yang.

The girl is smart and domineering.

Domineering is good. I need someone to keep an eye on him.

The bride was ever so slightly cross-eyed at the time of her marriage, which was rather attractive in an unconventional way. But she grew more and more so with age.

People recalled the adage that the cross-eyed had a penchant for evil. She did indeed try to frighten Third Uncle's wife when she was pregnant.

A devil with a beard ran inside the vestibule during the storm last night.

This is a sure sign that evil will come to newborns!

136

In her first few years at the House of Yang, Second Uncle's wife managed to hold her tongue, but as time went on, her husband's Taoist and slovenly ways rubbed off on her.

As the saying goes, "Husband and wife, over time, begin to stink alike," so she had taken to behaving like her husband but without quite his charm.

She had also grown increasingly bold after the birth of a son . . .

for a boy child gave her greater status.

Grandfather eyed Second Uncle's Wife from the vantage of the kang.

When guests come, you must keep your children away from my chambers.

They screech like wild animals.

Children grow little legs, which can't very well be tied up with ropes!

I didn't tell you to tie them up!

They must abide by the house rules!

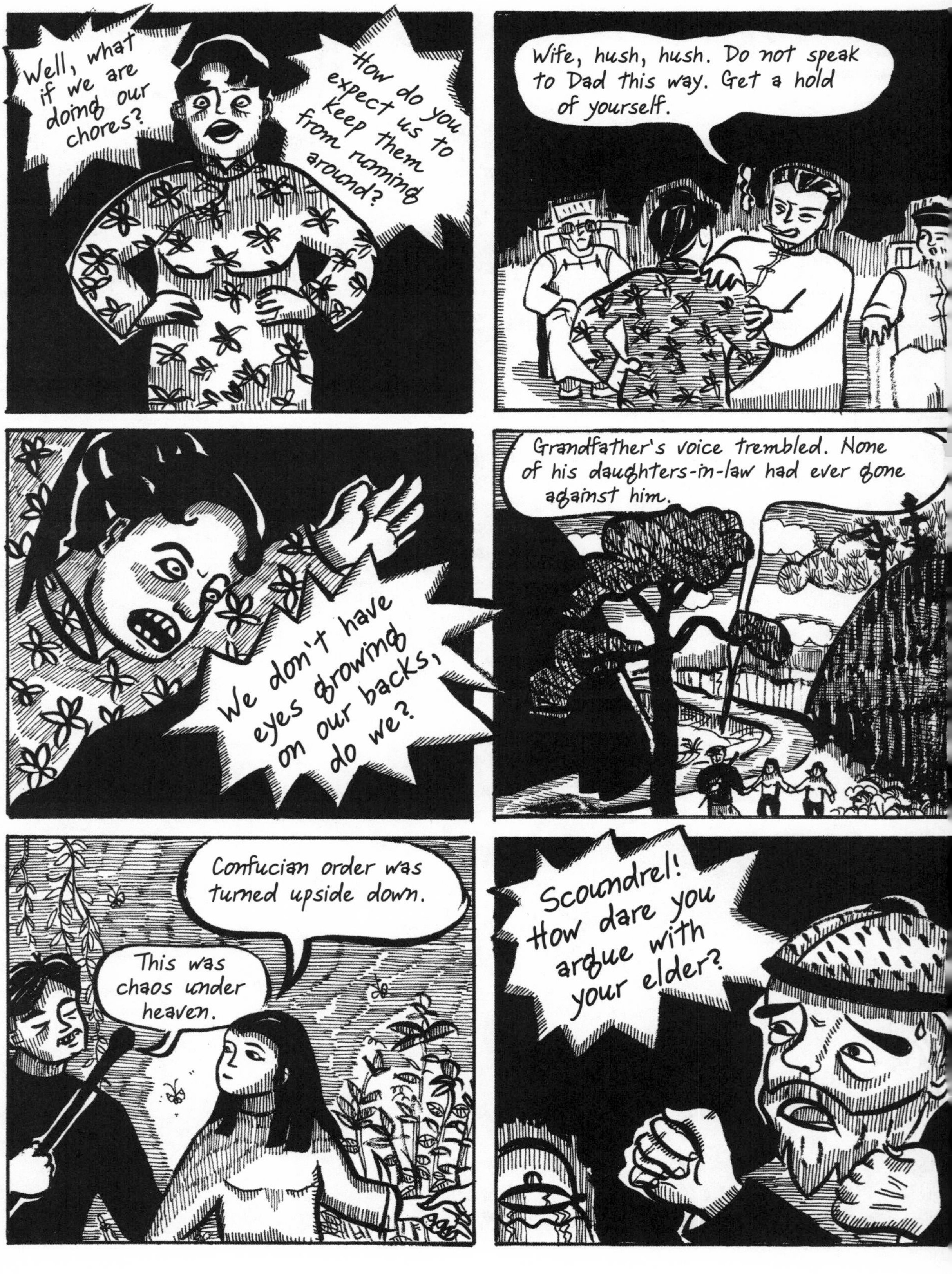
Well, what if we are doing our chores?
How do you expect us to keep them from roaming around?
Wife, hush, hush. Do not speak to Dad this way. Get a hold of yourself.
We don't have eyes growing on our backs, do we?
Grandfather's voice trembled. None of his daughters-in-law had ever gone against him.
Confucian order was turned upside down.
This was chaos under heaven.
Scoundrel! How dare you argue with your elder?

The real reason for the war between Grandfather and Second Uncle's Wife had to do with her breastfeeding.

It was a topic too uncomfortable and dangerous to bring to the surface.

Grandfather had always disapproved of women nursing babies outside their own chambers, especially with so many hired hands on the property.

Yet whenever her baby fussed, she sprung a breast out to quiet the child.

You get her to be more discreet, will you?

The Matriarch instructed her repeatedly but to no avail. The woman continued to flop out a breast in public.

139

Second Uncle's Wife continued to wear a terrible smirk of challenge.

Grandfather made a motion for his gun.

He always kept it on the kang against bandits.

Don't be angry, Father.

The women, with a flurry of hands, hustled the screaming woman out of the room.

Grandfather had asked the matchmaker for a daughter-in-law who could manage his errant son, but he had found one interested in managing him.

140

The subsequent family council dwindled to just Grandfather, Father and Father's new daughter-in-law.

Since the two men felt residual anger from their fight, the breakup of the family council became inevitable.

After Third Uncle reached the countryside in the autumn of 1944, the supplies sent back were small. It was as predicted: Third Uncle was stingy with the harvest.

He sent the usual amount of refined white flour, red beans for the Spring Festival jam, glutinous rice and white rice for Grandfather's table.

The rest of the family only had sorghum to eat.

Grandfather doesn't know we are eating so poorly.

No one wanted to complain to the Patriarch, lest he be accused of criticizing the old man for his decision to give Third Uncle control of the land.

It's Number Three's first year in the country. He needs to keep a lot of seed grain for next year.

Perhaps.

He has livestock to feed.

Greedy bastard.

Let's be patient. By next fall, things will get better.

That pig!

There had been severe shortages throughout Manchuria since the Japanese attack on Pearl Harbor in 1941.

Korea
Formosa
French Indochina
Dutch East Indies
Burma
Malaya

The Japanese occupiers enforced strict rationing on foodstuffs and cotton. Raw materials and manufactured goods were sent to supply their far-flung and overextended armies.

In the spring of 1945, the family focused on the news of the Pacific War. They listened to the broadcast from distant Chongqing on Fourth Uncle's radio.

Japanese units are being transferred by their desperate leadership

In May, we learned of the German surrender.

In August, Stalin sent one and a half million Red Army soldiers into Manchuria in a massive offensive against the Japanese.

We soon heard through word of mouth that atomic bombs had been dropped on Japan.

HWOONG

The Manchurians welcomed the Soviets as saviors . . .

. . . but the Red Army had come to loot and pillage, dragging what they could of Japanese factories, power stations and other infrastructure into the Soviet Union.

The Soviets facilitated the surrender of the Japanese to the Chinese Communists, known to the populace as the Eighth Route Army.

When the season turned chilly, the Nationalist troops of the Central Government under Chiang Kai-shek, helped by the Americans, finally arrived.

The Eighth Routers seeped back into the countryside.

The Nationalists took over the major cities and the railways linking them.

The coming of the Nationalists resuscitated hope.

May we have better days from now on.

Clink

Clink

Let's hope so.

Father had been living a string of sullen days at the House of Yang. Unless Grandfather summoned him to entertain guests, he did not leave his apartment.

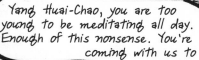

In the late summer of 1945, two old friends he had known from his turbulent days in Tianjin arrived at the House of Yang.

I've not seen you two in fourteen years.

Yang Huai-Chao, you are too young to be meditating all day. Enough of this nonsense. You're coming with us to Shenyang.

We are back from Chongqing to oversee the Japanese surrender.

The Central Government is short on men of talent to fill vacancies.

That's just what you need. Why don't you go to Shenyang? It'll do you good to get away from the tension here.

Well, I'll go on the condition that I won't be forced into any position of management. I want something leisurely.

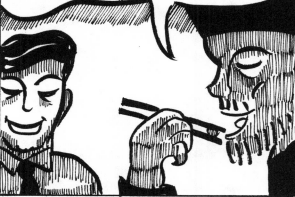

145

Don't worry, I promise you work that won't break a sweat.

Ha ha ha ha Ha ha

Father duly moved into a Japanese-style house in Shenyang. He set up his personal shrine to Buddha and began the life of an ascetic.

In the fall of 1945, I enrolled at the Shenyang Polytechnic, where I was a boarder during the week. I would visit Father on Saturday afternoons, before going home to Xinmin by train.

Soldiers packed the streets.

I took a shortcut to Father's house through a neighboring park. It was a rare sanctuary in a time of unrest.

The sun was setting. The evening grew cold.

I hear singing . . . a man and a woman.

The cover of darkness afforded the lovers privacy to give full voice to their emotions.

It's the love song about the tryst of the cowherd and the weaving maid.

When I walked through the cypresses and reached the edge of the lake, the song came to an end.

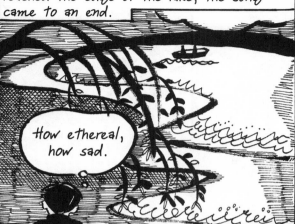

How ethereal, how sad.

Are they singing to welcome change, or is the song their farewell for the old way of life? Or are they simply in love and oblivious to the chaos?

Father was at home, deep in meditation.

He would open his eyes and look at me, then close his eyes again without a word.

When I returned to Xinmin, I immediately sought my mother.

Father was meditating. He's fine.

If your father is happy, I'm happy. Tell him next time, there's no need for him to make a trip home to check on us. We'll do just fine under this roof as long as we don't quarrel with others.

We have enough to eat.

I bit my tongue and nodded.

Mother, you poor, sweet soul. Don't you know he is unaware of our problems? Don't you know he doesn't care?

The Spring Festival of 1946 in Xinmin was worse than the year before. There were no treats to mark the New Year celebrations.

In good years, these would have been stacked high to honor the household gods.

福

There were only cabbages and turnips. I ate so many turnips, I thought I would turn into a turnip.

On the third day of the New Year, cigarette-puffing Second Uncle and secretive Fourth Uncle were invited to celebrate at Grandfather's table.

Second Uncle presented himself in the full splendor of his slovenliness.

Tsk. Just look at him. That's what has become of the fine fox coat I gave him.

I'm getting out of here before trouble begins.

I've got to go, Dad. I'm not well.

cough

cough cough

Second Uncle had not come in direct conflict with Grandfather over control of family land, but there was unspoken tension between them.

Dad is growing old and foolish.

Huai-Zhi blames me as much as Huai-Chao.

Grandfather had overlooked Second Uncle's bad habits when their relationship had been good.

Now that the relationship had fissures, he was reminded of Uncle's cross-eyed demon of a wife and his unruly children.

149

Second Uncle was oblivious to Grandfather's anger. Perhaps he pretended not to notice.

Dad, forget your worries and your sorrows.

Now, what's Huai-Zhi going to say to me?

Ahhh, good whiskey.

Dad, you must be like the chrysanthemums you love so much. You've got to be able to bear up in the cold.

So, you are reprimanding me, are you?

You, who rival Liu Bang of the Han Dynasty!

You're worst of the lot.

Dad, you compare me to Liu Bang. In what way am I like him?

LIU BANG WAS HAN DYNASTY'S FIRST EMPEROR, BUT BEFORE THAT HE WAS A BANDIT—A THUG! YOU TELL ME WHICH ASPECT OF THE MAN YOU MOST RESEMBLE!

Reeling from the blunt force of his father's words, Second Uncle left the apartment.

I was eating a frugal holiday meal when I spied Second Uncle staggering out from Grandfather's apartment.

When gray hair presses one to age and the New Year forces out the old...*

*Tang Dynasty poem.

I have never heard the man sing with such abandon, even when drunk. There is regret and bitterness in his voice. Is the song meant for Grandfather to hear?

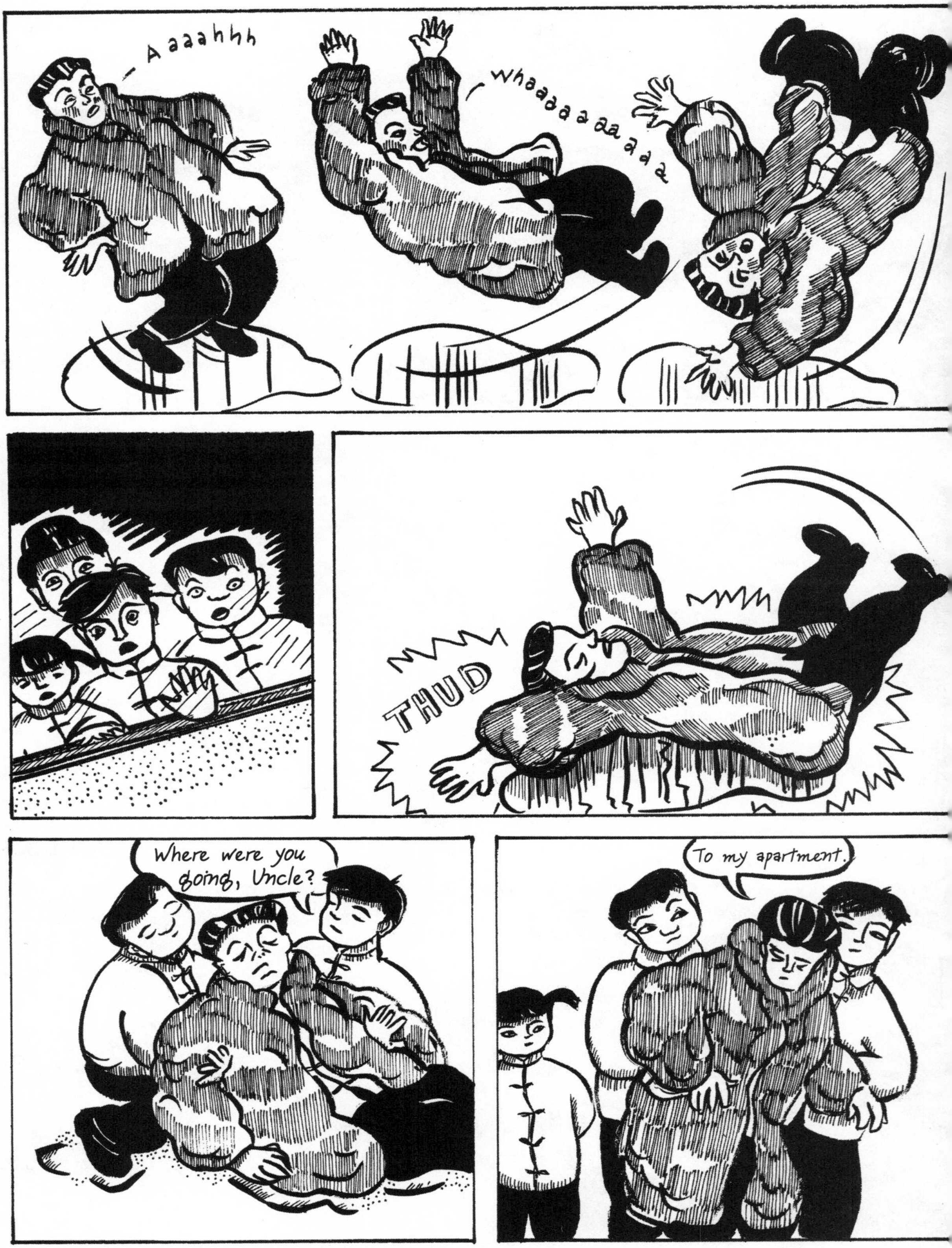
Aaaahhh
Whaaaaaaaaaaaa
THUD
Where were you going, Uncle?
To my apartment.

My uncle was so upset from his encounter with Grandfather, he was headed in the wrong direction.

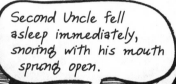

Second Uncle fell asleep immediately, snoring with his mouth sprung open.

I hear a motorcycle approaching.

VROOM

VROOM VROOM

VROOM

VROOM

VROOM

IT'S HIM!

It can't be Rotten Egg here.

VROOM

VROOM

VROOM

VRUM

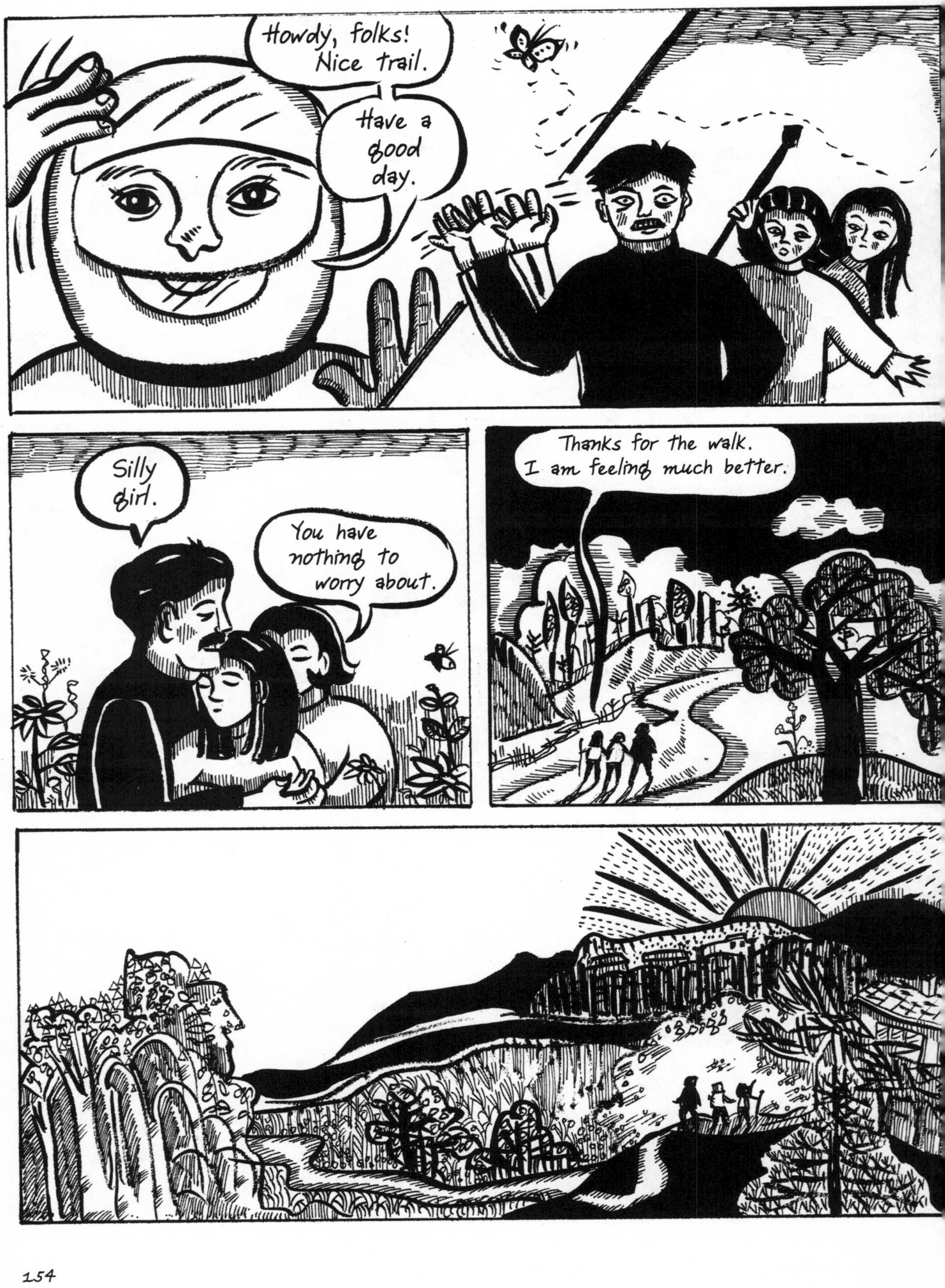
Howdy, folks! Nice trail.
Have a good day.
Silly girl.
You have nothing to worry about.
Thanks for the walk. I am feeling much better.

That's a good likeness of Third Uncle.

I love the comics format.

Indeed.

See, Baba, I met Third Uncle's son back in the winter of 1987. I'm using a photo of him as a model for his dad.

He was buying chemical fertilizer in Pan Jin from your brother. He wouldn't let me go with him into the countryside, because he said it was too rough for an American.

He does resemble his dad. Third Uncle was greedy, but he was not mean. Third Uncle fought with Father, but he didn't hold a grudge against me.

I went to visit him in Shantuozi the winter of 1946.

PHOTOS

Why did you go there? Did your father ask you to spy?

That's an insult! I would never spy. I was fond of him.

I went to Shantuozi every chance I got. The countryside was a lot more fun than Xinmin.

During the month of First Moon, I made my way out to the countryside. The wagon crossed the frozen river Liu.

We threaded our way through the dunes and scrub willows, passing villages whose inhabitants tended watermelon in summertime.

This area is swarming with bandits again. Some call themselves Eighth Routers.

Yes, they are also known as Communists. They say they will take from the rich and give to the poor.

That's right. These new sort of bandits are as hard to catch for the authorities as will-o'-the-wisps.

The silence is eerie.

There it is!

156

As the wedge of sun disappeared into the snowy field, the crows returned home to Granddaddy Hill, as if summoned by a silent call. Sometimes they startled and the whole lot of them again took flight.

Just look at that! There will be men of promise in the Yang Clan. See the crows circling like a ring of fog. The fengshui masters say vapors rising from one's ancestral burial grounds promise a glorious future.

I knew, of course, the wagoner was only saying what he thought a boy from a prominent family would want to hear.

The very first Yang who came to Manchuria is buried there.

Your granddad, Yang Junchen, is a good man. Built schools for the kids and did lots of good deeds. Hasn't forgotten his roots.

We're both natives of Shantuozi, but he's left for the city and made it big. Me, I'm still tied to this soil. Been working the land all my life.

But we have all got to come back to our birthplace. Fall leaves must return to the root of the tree.

I had no doubt Grandfather would fulfill his wish for a final return to the ancestral burying grounds, to nap for an eternity in the shade of the cypresses.

Ruddy Third Uncle boomed his welcome with genuine warmth, despite the unhappiness between him and Father.

Great to have you here, Zu-Wu!

As always, his eyes lingered on me, as if trying to see how tall his dead son, Little Autumn, would have been.

Because the Yang clan was highly esteemed for its philanthropy during times of flooding, drought and locusts, the village leaders pressed Third Uncle to become magistrate.

Men of wealth and scholarship were honored with this title, but it was an entirely voluntary position without pay.

A dozen men, paid full salaries, worked under him as bodyguards. Third Uncle loved the trappings of power.

In the unstable days after the Japanese surrender, as bandit groups made their return, his men carried rifles and Third Uncle never went without a gun under his coat.

Baldy, my second cousin, and I looked for adventures. I had a chance to play with guns, banned under the Japanese.

We ventured outside the village gates.

Don't go too far outside the gates, you two. The bandits will kill you if they want your guns.

The perimeter of Shantuozi had recently been fortified with the stout trunks of willow and tamped mud.

baaa
baaaabaaa baabaaaa

Up on Granddaddy Hill, the villagers hung a bronze temple bell. When lookouts spotted bandits, they sounded the alarm, brought in the sheep and shut the gate.

dang!
dang!
dang!
dang!
dang!
dang!
dang!

One morning, Baldy and I saw four mounted bandits. I had been told that if they meant no harm, they would dismount at the sound of gunfire.

We each fired a single round. The men slid off their horses and walked. We scurried back through the gate.

Bang! Bang

After a month in the countryside, I returned to Xinmin . . .

. . . then back to Shenyang for school and to see Father.

What's it like for Third Uncle out there?

Third Uncle has a nice life.

How so?

Well, lots of Third Uncle's friends came every evening to tell stories. Some even fell asleep and did not leave until morning. The kang was always toasty warm.

Anything else?

Uncle enjoys hunting and he likes to gamble in the local lottery.

What did they eat in Shantuozi?

Lots of meat and mung bean noodles, roasted peanuts, popcorn, fried sorghum tea and tobacco. There was plenty of food.

I felt awful. I loved to visit my relatives. If I went back to visit Third Uncle again, I'd feel as if I were indeed a spy.

No wonder Baba was so irritated when I teased him about spying.

I was angry that Father was turning me into an informer, collecting information to use against his third brother.

Children should never be turned into tools and weapons of parents.

Mreow

Since the Soviets had absconded with the transformers, Fourth Uncle had not been able to listen to the radio or eavesdrop on Grandfather.

He took over units east of Second Uncle's apartment on Market Street and began selling his treasures.

People brought him broken clocks and instruments to be fixed.

When he needed specialized tools and mechanical parts, not found in Xinmin, he called on me.

Zu-Wu, could you please buy fine machine oil in Shenyang?

Now that I was sixteen and no longer the nuisance who ruined his naps, he was deferential.

...

Like some tea?

Zu-Wu, when you come home on the weekends, I've got an extra room for you here. There's plenty of wood for heating.

At the same time, you can help me watch over the place. Keep an eye out for thieves coming in from the streets and your second uncle's pilfering kids.

Hee he

I preferred the room behind Fourth Uncle's shop to mine. The Nationalists had no barracks, so the people of Xinmin were forced to billet the soldiers.

Let's roast their chickens.

Fourth Uncle's Shop

At the House of Yang, they were put up in the front apartments. Some were encamped in the yard. It had become too noisy for me to study in my old room.

One evening after returning from school in Shenyang, I tried to study but could not concentrate.

The reeds rustled *swa-swa-swa*. The maples I had planted as a child clamored *ga-la-ga-la-ga-la* in the breeze. The pavilion was in neglect, its thatch roof grown black with mold.

The shadow of weasels slithering along the edge of the trench gave me shivers.

I went to pay my respects to my favorite, Second Uncle, living next door in disarray.

Zu-Wu, you're a scholar, do you know what it means by "*wu yu nai gang*"?

It means if you have no desires, you're as strong as steel?

There's more to it.

Zhuangzi, the Taoist master of the fourth century BC, was told that the king wanted to confer a title and office upon him.

gurgle gurgle

Zhuangzi replied, "I have no desire for a title and office, my good man."

Have you seen the bull they display at the temple during the holidays at the temple?

That bull had been fed the best grass, but his entrails are dug out, and then they dress him in a brocade cape and sacrifice him to the gods.

If I were to accept the king's offer, I'd end up like that bull. If I wanted to return to my simple way of life, I would no longer be able to do so.

If you are truly without desires, no one can force you to make kowtows.

Nephew, I wear shabby clothes the year round. If I owned one thousand outfits, I could still only wear one at a time.

If you don't need to beg a favor or dress up for an interview, how perfectly comfortable are your old clothes, eh?

Why own estates when you need no more than a three feet by six feet patch of space for sleep? Why would you want a thousand rooms?

Why not live this kind of life and be a free man?

Yes, you make a lot of sense, Uncle.

If you look into my hovel, even the reed mats I sleep on are full of holes.

Think of your granddad with so much land, a big house and many nice gowns.

He's always worried about this and that.

His clothes need airing because he's afraid of moths.

Nephew, you must learn from me and you will be happy, otherwise there is not much happiness to be had in the world.

But Uncle, I have many desires. After I graduate from the polytechnic, more than anything else, I want to attend university.

In the future, I want a pretty wife. When I meet her, I can't court her in shabby clothes. I can't invite her to live in a hovel. I can't live entirely without desires.

You can do it. One small step after another will help you achieve peace in this life. Don't let your desires make you their slave.

SWOOSH

In the summer of 1946, Second Uncle followed Fourth Uncle's example and set up shop, too. But he had nothing so fine as clocks and musical instruments to sell.

Now everyone in Xinmin was witness to a son of the House of Yang turned watermelon vendor.

Hey, old master, come and have a slice of melon.

That fourth son of old Yang Junchen is doing pretty well for himself. He's opened up a nice, clean shop full of clocks and things.

Yes, but that second son of the old man . . . tsk! He used to have a job at the Bank of Manchuria. Just like a beggar now.

167

Brother, sit down, it's of no consequence if you don't have money. My melons won't cost you anything. If you are thirsty, help yourself!

Old master, where have you come from?

From Wang Village or Li Hamlet, they would say, and Second Uncle would prod them for news of activities in the countryside.

He learned the situation was relatively stable with the Nationalists in control of the cities and the Communists in control of the countryside.

There was no power after the Soviets absconded with the transformers, so newspapers could not be published.

But the depth and breadth of the news that Second Uncle was able to gather was extraordinary. He was well apprised of gossip too. He was Xinmin's living newspaper.

Grandfather was so ashamed of Second Uncle's activities, he started to avoid Market Street altogether.

Mother, how did he turn out like this? Just as Master Gao predicted.

Yes, he said if he goes bad, he will go very, very bad.

When I went to visit Second Uncle, he gave me melon to eat.

Nephew, I am not the Marquis of Donglin, but I'm selling his melons.

When the Qin Dynasty collapsed in 206 BC, a high official lost everything. He ended up outside the wall of the capital as a melon farmer.

He grew tired of poverty, so he went to visit a fortune-teller.

I used to be the Marquis of Donglin, now I am a mere melon farmer. Can you see a better future for me?

You are selling melons now because you attained the highest point in the cycle of fortune. Now the wheel has turned, and you are at the level you should be.

Count yourself lucky they didn't chop your head off when the last dynasty fell.

Shouldn't you be content to be alive to sell melons?

...

It is foolish for you to hope for the attainment of power again.

Well, that was one honest fortune-teller, wouldn't you say?

Probably went out of business quickly for such truths, Uncle.

In the fall of 1946, I continued to stay in the room behind Fourth Uncle's shop, but there was nothing for me to watch over.

I've sold all the best items...

...and bought gold.

With the melon season over in the fall of 1946, Second Uncle closed up shop and spent a lot of time in the North Garden.

One evening, I found him composing poetry while drinking from a chipped cup. He was snacking on dried tofu strips and dipping them in soy sauce, garlic and green onions.

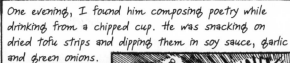

Ah, you've come, Zu-Wu. Here, have some tofu and mulled wine.

No, thank you, Uncle, I've just had dinner.

Zu-Wu, you're a scholar. What's your opinion of books?

Well ... they're useful, naturally.

Second Uncle ripped a velvety page out of an old book, and rolled it into a spill with which he lit the tobacco in his water pipe.

You did wrong. It's not a matter of money, Uncle, but that you've destroyed good books. Why would you do such a thing?

Aiya. These are valuable books, but if you hold on to them, you're always worried about bookworms chewing them.

My nephew, a book of one hundred pages— you're lucky to read ten pages of truth in it.

Think of it—ten—that's a darn good book. Most of the time, you get only a couple of useful sentences. The rest are simply wasted words.

If you're going to read a book, remember only the useful parts. Don't go putting any effort into retaining the nonsense.

Once you've finished reading, burn everything. The truth is, even the bits that make sense aren't really all that useful.

Don't take books too seriously. If you remember nothing, that's okay, too. It's all a lot of drivel.

Me—I'm not keeping books or anything else for that matter.

My coming into this world will mean the same as never having come at all. This life isn't real. It's all done in a flash of lightning, done like morning dew.

Winter of 1947. I was home in Xinmin for the holidays. It was so bitterly cold, spit landed on the ground with a crack.

Fourth Uncle's door leading to Market Street was always locked now that he had sold all his treasures.

The emptiness I found inside his store was not unusual, but the emptiness that confronted me in the North Garden was staggering.

The two columns of mature maples, which I had planted years ago on Arbor Day, had been cut down.

Beneath those trees, which I had lovingly pruned and fertilized, I had dreamed my dreams. Beneath them, a child in a large, noisy family had found solace.

It didn't take me long to find maple logs piled up against Second Uncle's wall.

Second Uncle's apartment was toasty warm.

Second Uncle studied my contorted face.

Uncle, how could you cut down the trees I planted?

Sit down, Zu-Wu, sit down near the brazier.

The units in the front have been destroyed by the soldiers. They tear down the doors and the fine latticework and burn them.

The thatched pavilion is no more. The trees, which you planted and took care of, didn't you once enjoy their beauty? Isn't that enough for you?

If you find your second uncle sitting here shivering and shriveling into his jacket, will that make you happy?

I had to smile at the pathetic image he was painting. I remembered how knobby his knees looked in summer as he played melon vendor.

brr   brr   brr

With the Communists and Nationalists misfiring mortar shells into our gardens, do you still have the heart to contemplate their beauty?

BOOM BANG PING

Now that the days are bitter, you and I can enjoy the warmth they provide.

How useful your maples, so why feel sad that I've cut them down?

We don't know if next year we'll still have this garden. Why hoard property and later be accused of being a rich man?

I was now without anger. I suddenly felt sorry for Second Uncle, noticing that the thinness of his body could not be hidden under winter clothes.

I sat down on the warm kang, calmly listening to Second Uncle expound on his philosophy of life.

I need to make my own mistakes to learn, Baba.

A smart person learns from the mistakes of others.

Don't be so hard on her. You made one mistake after another in trusting people, Zu-Wu.

You were well into your forties.

And then when we moved to Carmel, you were softhearted and were made a fool by the same person.

Each time, we were turned out to starve!

She's right.

Thanks, Mom.

During Chinese holidays, when there is plenty on the table, Baba always gets misty-eyed. I know he is thinking of his youth when there was no food.

I AM HUNGRY

177

That winter of 1946-47, the Communists were increasingly active in the countryside.

They fought into Shantuozi from the north, the heavy willow trunk barriers unable to keep them out.

The villagers did not understand who was attacking. Perhaps just another bandit uprising, they thought. But these bandits fired machine guns and threw grenades.

Magistrate! The bandits are coming after you.

In the confusion, Third Uncle became separated from his family.

He managed to reach the village of Second Terrace. He did not notice he had lost his shoes.

Kinsmen soaked his feet in warm water, wrapped them in pieces of sheepskin, and put him on a horse.

We can't keep him here. The Communists will come after us.

At the House of Yang, we had just finished breakfast.

How strange. The dark figure does not dismount . . .

It's Third Uncle!

Quick! Get a basin of cold water for his feet. Get Doctor Yang!

At Second Terrace they soaked my feet in warm water.

Dr. Yang was the son of my grandfather's eldest brother, who had gambled away the family land and property.

Grandfather had supported this cousin until he became an established doctor of Chinese medicine.

Huai-Lian, the damage is severe, made worse by soaking in warm water.

Two months later:

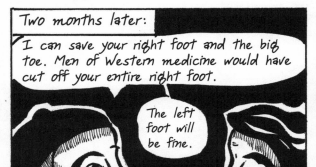

I can save your right foot and the big toe. Men of Western medicine would have cut off your entire right foot.

The left foot will be fine.

It did not take very long to remove the gangrenous toes, for they were ready to fall off.

GAhh.

Now this foot will be safe.

Grandfather repeatedly reached for his tea.

Sigh.

A month later, the wound had closed and Third Uncle was able to hobble about with a cane.

With the loss of four of his toes, there was no spring in his steps.

What happened to his wife and kids?

Two weeks after he fled, he received a message from his wife, saying they were safe in Zhangwu where his wife's parents lived.

Soon the hoodlums in Shantuozi, with encouragement from the Communists, looted his house.

They led away the livestock.

They carted away the grain in the silos, and the rice hidden beneath the sheepfold.

The Communists did not defend territory. They stayed long enough to manipulate the criminal elements as recruits and frighten the people.

You have committed grave crimes. Come with us. We will protect you.

Villagers who had taken part in the looting, but were too old to join the Communists, feared reprisal.

The magistrate will send the Nationalists after us.

They came trotting over to Xinmin, sobbing, as they begged forgiveness.

It wasn't me who stole your grain, your honors.

Me—I didn't take a thing, sir.

Now, had Third Uncle been generous to his family in Xinmin, they would still have food.

In his second year, he had kept nearly all the harvest.

In one raid, all was gone.

It was the bleakest Spring Festival in memory. In the previous year we were worried that there were no New Year Eve's dumplings. This year, we were fighting with the mice for the grain fallen beneath the floorboards.

Scram! Rats!

Shenyang was now under siege by the Communists and railway lines were often impassable.

In the new year of 1947, I had no money for tuition. When I managed to ride the train to Shenyang, I looked in on my classmates.

We miss you.

Grandfather has too much to think about without me asking for money.

Father is as emotionally remote as ever.

How can I possibly ask for tuition when at home the women and children are fighting mice for anything to eat?

It's not worth asking Father to see his neck thicken as he doles out the cash.

But it's time to visit him for Mother's peace of mind.

Third Uncle's toes had to come off. He cried when the Doctor Yang removed them to keep his entire foot from rotting.

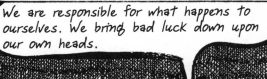We are responsible for what happens to ourselves. We bring bad luck down upon our own heads.

It is only the beginning for Huai-Lian.

If he does not change his course, his days of suffering are still ahead of him.

Father spoke calmly, not in anger or hate, just matter-of-factly—but his words made me shiver.

When Xinmin also came under siege, it was even more difficult for grain to reach us.

Father is fine, Mother. It's easier to get food in Shenyang. It's time to worry about us.

Mother had to sell the earrings her own mother had made for her when she became a bride to buy food.

What, Mother? Were you saving those for my future bride?

Mother continued to weep noisily into her handkerchief in spite of my joke.

Grandfather had plenty of cash to buy grain on the black market. Fourth Uncle and his wife wormed their way to the elder's table.

At night, I could hear the roar of cannons and the sound of gunfire as Xinmin came under attack.

POW

Boom

TA-TA-TA-TA

When the food Mother bought with the earrings ran out . . .

Wait, why didn't your grandfather feed the rest of you?

Only the comfort of my grandparents mattered.

In our youths, adults ate the meatballs and the kids the remaining cabbages. Children came last. Grandparents had seniority.

No one would have dreamed of buying you a car at sixteen under the old system.

Yeah, I was spoiled.

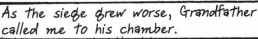

As the siege grew worse, Grandfather called me to his chamber.

Zu-Wu, find out if the trains are running. If so, we'll go see our kinsmen, the Jins in Shenyang, about housing.

It is getting too dangerous here.

Days later, I escorted Grandfather, Grandmother and Youngest Aunt from Xinmin to Shenyang.

When Third Uncle's wife arrived in Xinmin with their two children from Zhangwu, we learned how much worse it was in the countryside.

Sister-in-Law, we have to boil this sweater to kill the lice.

Soon, I also escorted Third Uncle's family by wagon and train to Shenyang.

Doggies on roof!

The toddler who pointed at the statuaries on the temple roof is the same cousin you met trucking fertilizer from Panjing to Zhangwu.

When I had taken care of Third Uncle's family, it was time to escort Mother and three younger siblings to the relative safety of Shenyang.

When Father saw us at the door, he did not rise from meditation.

THERE IS FOOD AND HOUSING IN XINMIN!

WHY DO YOU BRING EVERYONE HERE?

I had never raised my voice to Father until this day.

HOW CAN YOU BE SO BLIND?

SHELLS LAND IN OUR GARDENS, FATHER, EVERY DAY. DON'T YOU UNDERSTAND?

IT'S NO TIME FOR YOU TO BE THINK-ING ONLY OF YOURSELF! OPEN YOUR EYES, FATHER!

THIS ISN'T THE TIME TO BE MEDITATING!

Father stared at me, as if seeing me for the very first time.

He has grown.

Good-bye, Mother.

I returned to Xinmin. My third brother and his new wife were nibbling on scarce cornmeal pancakes.

Yuan the Idiot said your brother was a goose in his former life.

Yes.

My third brother was not the adventurous sort.

Brother, go to Second Terrace where your in-laws live. They will have food.

You are not made for the city.

If I can make it to Nationalist-controlled Beijing, I may be able to attend a government-sponsored university for refugee students.

I left the next morning. My sister-in-law wept, for I had been the problem solver. Now she would have to rely on her honest but simple husband.

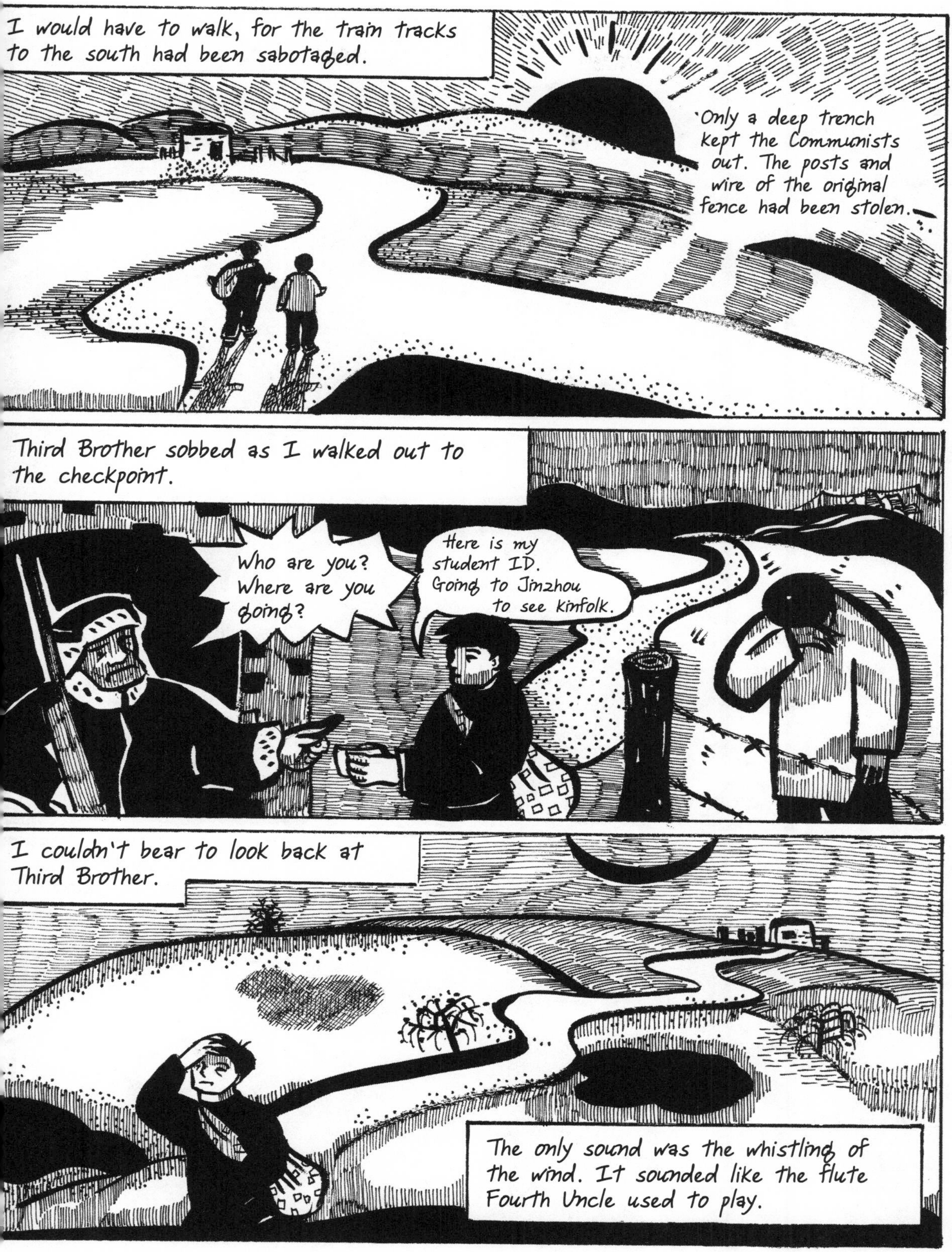
I would have to walk, for the train tracks to the south had been sabotaged.
Only a deep trench kept the Communists out. The posts and wire of the original fence had been stolen.
Third Brother sobbed as I walked out to the checkpoint.
Who are you? Where are you going?
Here is my student ID. Going to Jinzhou to see kinfolk.
I couldn't bear to look back at Third Brother.
The only sound was the whistling of the wind. It sounded like the flute Fourth Uncle used to play.

Baba, would you have left home if you knew your journey would be difficult?

Would I?

In Beijing, there was no university for refugee students. The Nationalists wanted to send us into the military.

NO CONSCRIPTION!!

東北同學會

The Nationalists shot us in the back when the protesters grew in number.

ta-ta-ta

Manchuria was taken by the Communists, and Beijing came under siege. It would be lost in January of 1949.

I have to go farther south.

In Shandong Province, I was detained once, robbed and imprisoned.

We know you're a spy!

You are a Communist!

By the time I arrived in Shanghai, I hadn't been able to bathe for four months and was put in a beggar's asylum.

They don't feed me enough. These crabs may be good.

190

When I heard the Communists had crossed the Yangtze, I left the asylum. The train was crammed with refugees. I couldn't move my legs for days.

Communists have crossed the Yangtze into the South.

The Gan River in Jiangsu had flooded. I tied myself to bamboo culms so I could rest.

The Communists pressed south. I crossed the Gan on a log. Many drowned in the attempt.

I was conscripted by the Nationalists in Canton and shipped to Taiwan, there to defend Chiang Kai-shek's island refuge . . .

but I escaped . . .

. . . and became a street person in Taipei, the capital, with no place to sleep.

Then I went deep into the mountains of the aborigines to teach Chinese to the children and contracted malaria.

Would I have left Manchuria if I knew my journey would be so tough?

No! Definitely not!

Baba, what if you knew you'd have a nice little family of your own, and end up in America, living peacefully by the sea?

Then the answer is YES!

I courted Laning and married her.

You were born in 1960 when your mother and I were both teaching in Taipei.

WHAAH!

In the sixties, we left the authoritarian island of Taiwan for Japan, which was now a democracy. There I attended graduate school.

We arrived in San Francisco during the civil rights movement and were sworn in as citizens in 1975.

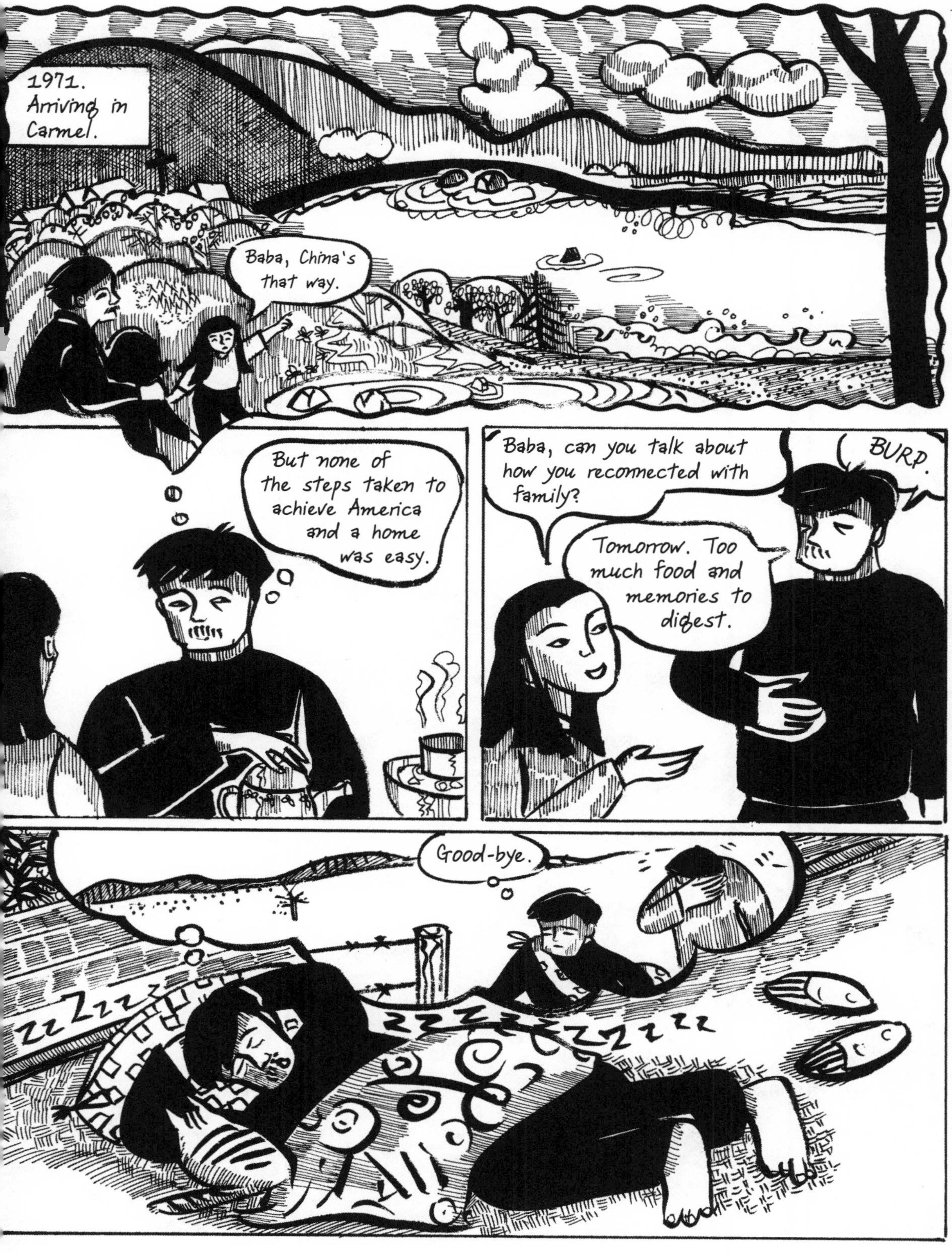
1971. Arriving in Carmel.
Baba, China's that way.
But none of the steps taken to achieve America and a home was easy.
Baba, can you talk about how you reconnected with family?
BURP.
Tomorrow. Too much food and memories to digest.
Good-bye.
ZZZZZZ
ZZZZZZZZZZZZZ

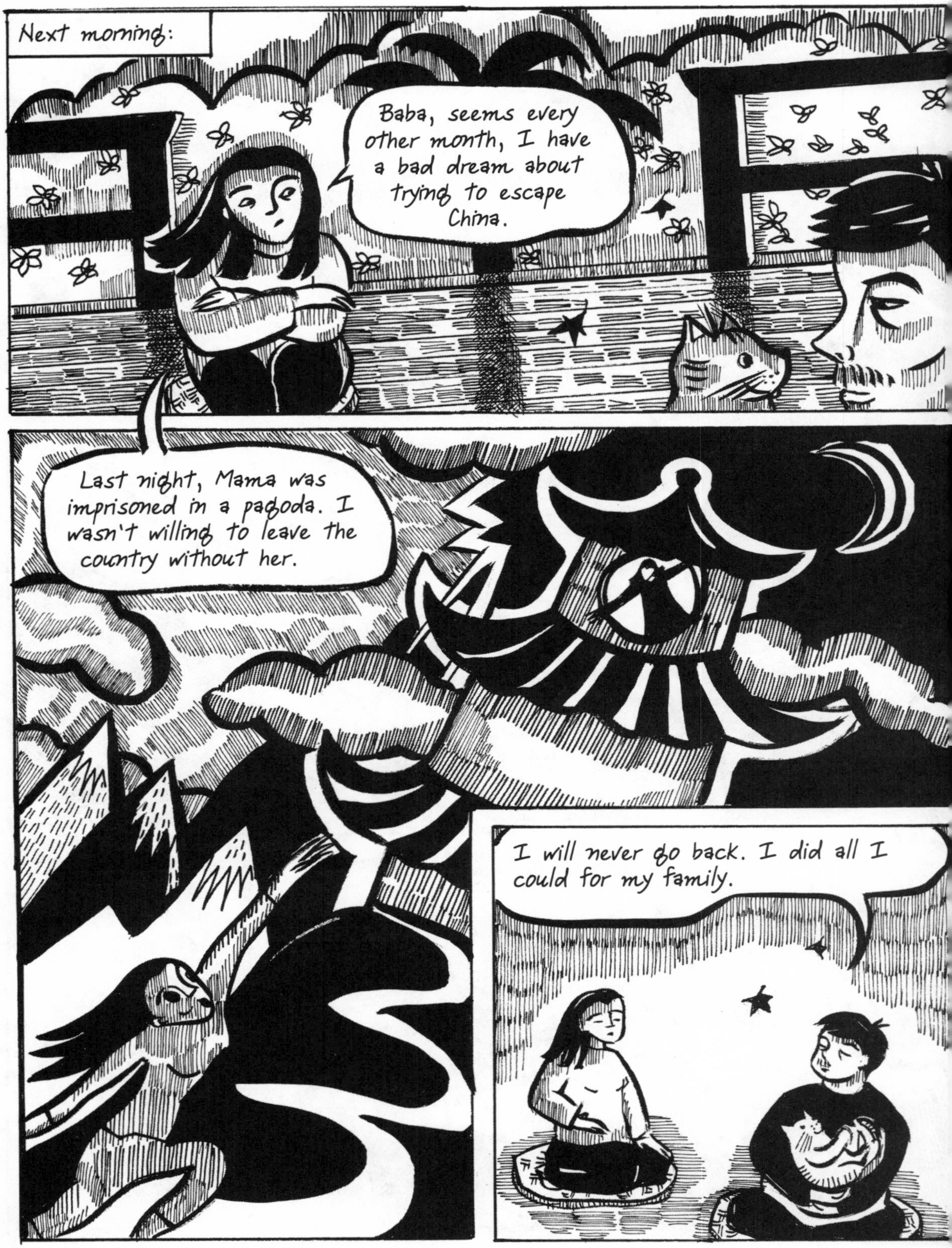
Next morning:
Baba, seems every other month, I have a bad dream about trying to escape China.
Last night, Mama was imprisoned in a pagoda. I wasn't willing to leave the country without her.
I will never go back. I did all I could for my family.

Soon after I landed in Tokyo for graduate school, I wrote home to Xinmin.

Japan had diplomatic ties with China?

Yes, but not normalization of relations.

I had drafted a long letter, but in the end I cut it down to only a few lines to say I was in Japan with wife and child.

I didn't want to endanger anyone by his connection to a foreigner. China had been shut to the West since 1949.

I waited and waited for a reply. Just as I was about to give up, a letter came from Father.

Yes, a letter from China, Yang-San!

"We are all fine. Your mother is fine. We are now living in Shenyang, not Xinmin."

He is afraid to write more.

So I began sending money to China, knowing that the country had just emerged from a famine, which took tens of millions of lives.

195

And in 1972, Nixon went to visit China!

In 1979, after normalizations of relations between the U.S. and China, I flew to Beijing then boarded a train for Shenyang. A return after thirty-one years.

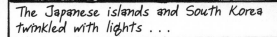

The Japanese islands and South Korea twinkled with lights . . .

. . . but when we entered Chinese air space, the land below was pitch black.

I knew China would be dreary, but I was shocked to fall into a sea of roiling dingy blue.

I'd taken sunglasses, ready to hide tears, but no tears came.

Here nephew, you like them, you have them.

My family swarmed around me like locusts.

I want a television set.

I want a fridge.

I want a Swiss watch.

I want to go to an American school.

I want a fur coat.

196

You adopt our son and educate him in America.

Our connections to you, a foreigner, ruined his chances for university.

Besides, you only have a daughter.

Hnh, the nerve..."you only have a daughter."

No one cared about my well-being. No one asked if my life abroad had been difficult.

The person I wished to see above all others was my mother.

Ma, do you know who I am?

That's your son.

?

I've waited so long to see her again, and now she's gone.

Your hands are so soft.

I'm not a farmer, Ma.

My father was as selfish as ever.

Why are you spending so much time with your brother? You came home to see me, didn't you?

197

My third brother, the one who accompanied me to the western checkpoint of Xinmin, was blind from malnutrition.

A family member stole the pair of leather dress shoes I had brought for my eldest brother.

Kinsmen tattled on one another, while the stories I wanted to hear—how the Patriarch lived and died—were shrouded in mystery.

I had planned to stay in China for a full month, but I left in a hurry after three weeks.

Welcome home, Mr. Yang.

Yes! America is my real home.

When your dad returned to this house, I filled a tub of water for him, and there he sat and wept long and hard.

I was too preoccupied with college and boyfriends to care about Baba . . .

I came home with unanswered questions, but from what my family did and did not say, I pieced together the stories.

It's not too late for me to get to know him.

In the winter of 1948, Shenyang was taken by the Communists. The Nationalists surrendered without much of a fight.

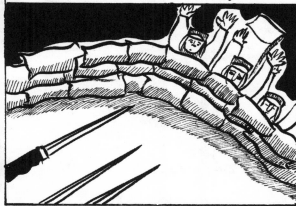

The conflict has ended. It is the beginning of a new society. From this day forward, a new era of equality and justice will dawn . . .

Third Uncle reading a Communist wall poster.

Everyone, landowners or peasants, must return to his native town or village.

Daddy, are we gonna be okay?

The Communists have no quarrel with me. I didn't rent land, I merely hired peasants to work. I didn't exploit anyone.

And they say they welcome former landowners.

Having nothing on his conscience, Third Uncle decided it was safe to return to ancestral Shantuozi with his family. Grandmother joined her favorite son.

She did not go to Xinmin with Grandfather and Second Aunt to check on the estate, because she wanted to see how her siblings were faring in neighboring Zhoutuozi.

That spring, Father left Shenyang, and Second Uncle departed from Xinmin with their families for Shantuozi, their place of birth.

They knew of no other way to feed their families except by farming.

As soon as they arrived, they fell under the surveillance of the newly formed Peasant Association.

Every day feels like pig slaughter day!

At least the pigs get to squeal zrr-zrr-zrr.

The quieter the days, the more frightening.

Men from the Peasant Association did finally come for Third Uncle. They forced him limping into a one-room hut.

You are brought here before the representatives of the poor and oppressed.

They made Father and Second Uncle watch.

They knew just where to hit to inflict the greatest injury without killing a man.

Yang Huai-Lian is sentenced to twenty years of reform through labor in Tongliao!

When Third Uncle lost consciousness, they tossed him into the back of a wagon with other prisoners.

My Third Uncle was convicted for being a rich landowner, having appropriated vast fields and forests.

When my grandmother heard her favorite son had been trussed up like a hog and carted off, she suffered a stroke and died that very day.

They wrapped her body, light as a rabbit, in a rush mat . . .

. . . and buried her on top of Granddaddy Hill.

At the labor camp, Third Uncle lasted eight months.

He was buried in a mass grave.

Father and Second Uncle waited for the men to come for them next, but they had not been landlords.

Those destined for labor camp had been carted away. Those to be executed had been shot outside the village. They breathed a sigh of relief.

Under land redistribution, the two families were given alkaline soil as hard as rock which, during the summer, turned into yellow soup.

In the first year, each man's land produced only enough to feed him and his family for four months.

Mother, I can see the bottom of the bin.

It looks bad for grown men to go begging. You and I go instead, eh, sister-in-law?

Hmph, Men are so brittle.

It was decided Second Uncle's Wife and Mother would make the rounds with grain sacks to the peasant families with more productive land.

Brrr...

Sister, I keep having this nightmare. When I was small, I went with my mother into the Great Eastern Wilds for firewood.

We were greedy for more, so we went deeper into the scrub. The sun was setting and we'd lost our way. We heard wolves.

The hungry animals came after us. Fortunately my brother called for us, and we followed his voice to safety.

Don't fret, Sister. It's only a dream, not a bad omen.

Villagers found the women shivering and stamping their feet at their wattle gate.

You're from the House of Yang? How'd you end up like this?

I remember the schools Yang Junchen built. I remember Yang Junchen talked to the government in a year of flood, and we were all exempted from taxes.

Here you go. Sorghum, maize and millet.

Daughter, give them wheat and rice and some black beans, too.

As the women trudged across a frozen stream, wind blowing sleet in their faces, Mother threw down her sack of grains.

This is too much! When I married into the Yang clan, I never thought I'd end up like this!

Sister, Sister, why be sad? What's there to worry about?

Look at all we were able to get. We'll have lots to eat. Can't you smell it already?

My son, Zu-Wu, has plain disappeared. I keep dreaming of standing in the road, waiting for him to come home.

He must have died. He was always too adventurous . . . remember the time he was stung by the wasps?

I had spotted their nest and stabbed it with my stick.

Haaii . . . children are like fingers of the hand. Take a bite of any finger and the hand will hurt.

They laughed at how absurdly and absolutely destitute they were. They could descend no lower. What more could they be afraid of?

At home the women made pancakes.

Brother, we can't very well lounge about, waiting for food to fall into our mouths.

We'll fetch kindling.

One day in spring, the brothers set out for the Great Eastern Wilds.

Look at those two, talking philosophy. They go for wood but bring back little.

Just a few sticks tied together with a length of rope.

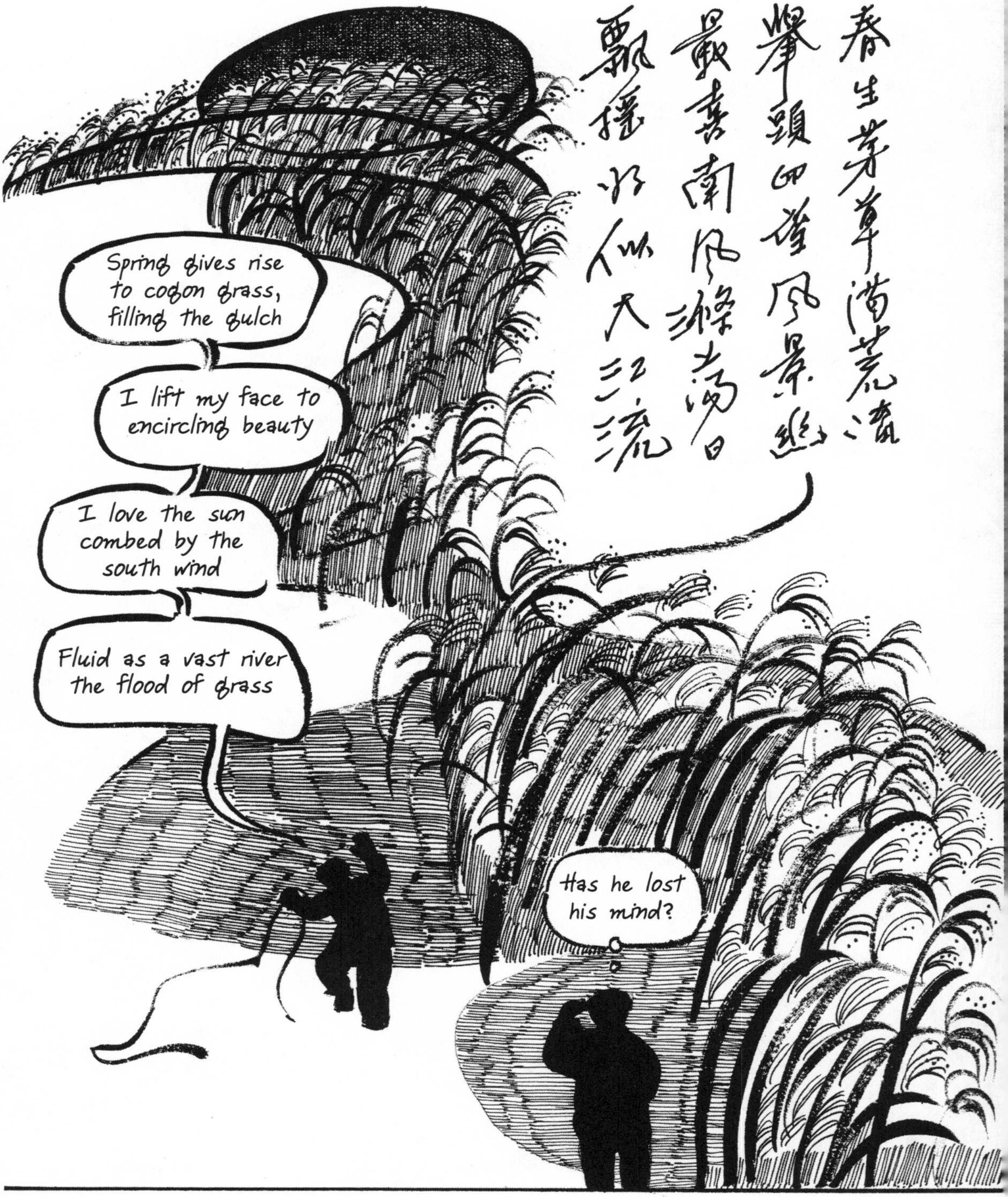
春生茅草滿荒溝
擧頭四望風景幽
最喜南風滌蕩日
飄搖好似大江流
Spring gives rise to cogon grass, filling the gulch
I lift my face to encircling beauty
I love the sun combed by the south wind
Fluid as a vast river the flood of grass
Has he lost his mind?

When I see such beauty, I feel as if I've disappeared.

I became part of the landscape.

How'd the poem get passed down to you, Baba?

When I visited my father, he recited it to me. I remembered it.

Later that spring, Second Uncle came to visit Father.

I'm not going to plant sorghum this year, brother. It needs too much work, what with furrowing.

Watermelons will save energy. All I'll have to do is take a hoe and make holes, put a few seeds in and kick dirt over them.

If I plant now, they'll be ready by midsummer. I'll be able to buy grain to eat from the money I'll make selling melons.

You sure you know what you're doing?

Yup!

Second Uncle attended market at Zhoutuozi and bought a sack of melon seeds.

209

He and his wife planted the seeds.

My watermelons are doing well. They're the size of chicken eggs.

A few weeks later:

The biggest melons are already the size of goose eggs.

But the melons grew no bigger.

Second Uncle and his wife brought a neighbor to inspect their patch.

Why don't our watermelons grow any bigger?

Because you didn't plant watermelons.

Hei? Why aren't they watermelons? I bought watermelon seeds.

What you've got are xiang yuan. They're only good for lookin' at.

In the past, people planted a few vines in their backyards to enjoy their greenery on summer eves.

There's certainly no market for melons that can't be eaten.

211

On an afternoon after heavy rain, Second Uncle went to his weed-grown melon patch and picked the roundest, ripest melon he could find.

Eldest Brother, I've harvested my melons and brought the largest for you!

He wiped it as lovingly as if it were a baby's bottom.

Tell me if this isn't the handsomest melon you've seen?

These three months have been a complete waste. My harvest is the color of sorrow.

I wanted to make you a gift of one, but I thought I should write you a poem to go with it.

Hai, Huai-Zhi, you've made such a mess of things, how can you be making poems?

Most of the farmers didn't think much of Father and Second Uncle after witnessing their wretched efforts, but a handful of villagers who had some schooling respected them all the same.

On New Year's Eve, peasants came visiting at Father's hut into the wee hours to pay their respects. Second Uncle had fallen asleep on Father's kang.

There was nothing to offer the guests, not even boiled water, but the talk fed the soul.

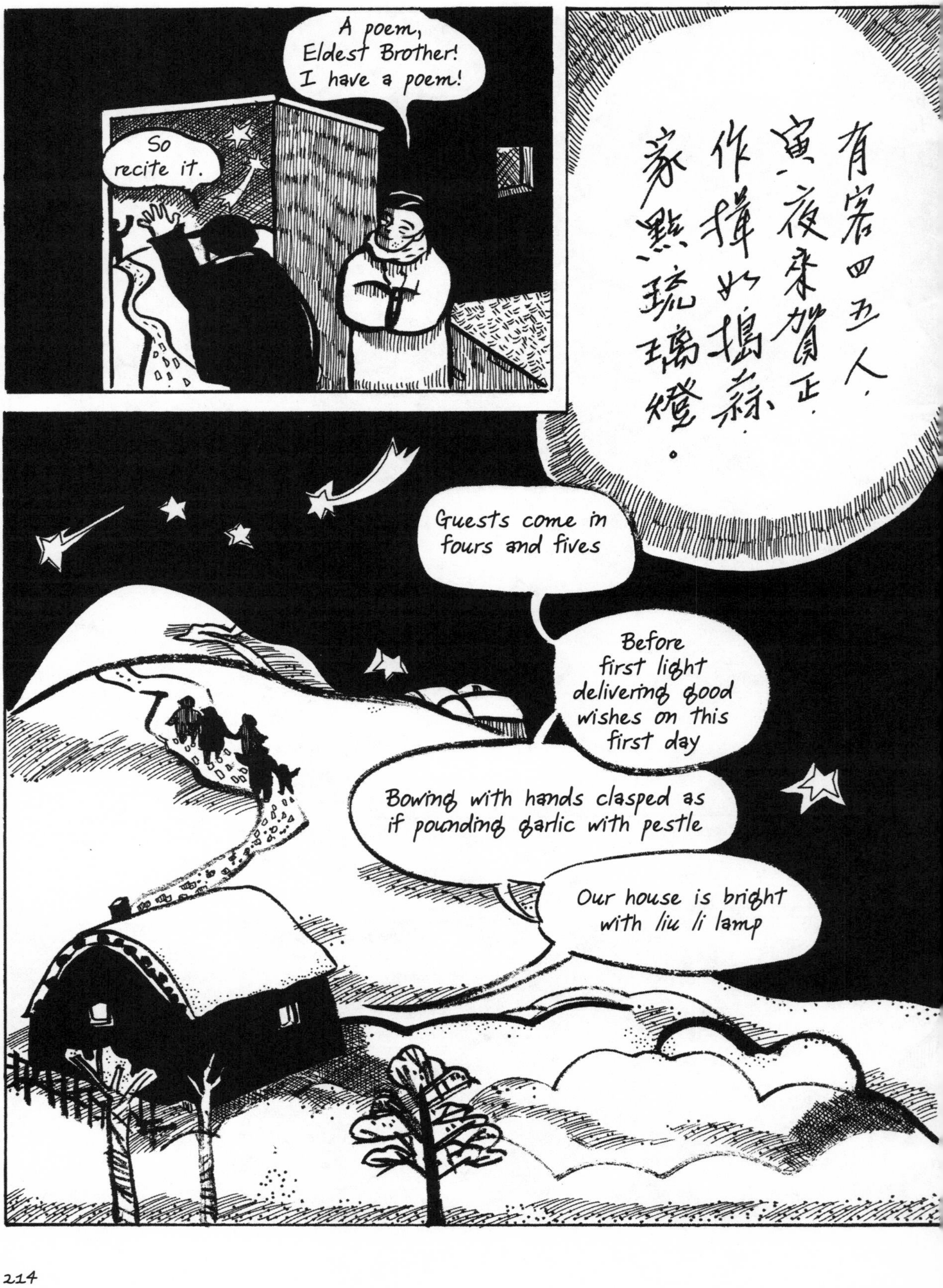
A poem, Eldest Brother! I have a poem!
So recite it.
有客四五人，
寅夜來賀正，
作揖如搗蒜，
家點琉璃燈。
Guests come in fours and fives
Before first light delivering good wishes on this first day
Bowing with hands clasped as if pounding garlic with pestle
Our house is bright with liu li lamp

You sure know how to talk nonsense. Our lamp is made from the bottom of a broken bottle with a string for a wick.

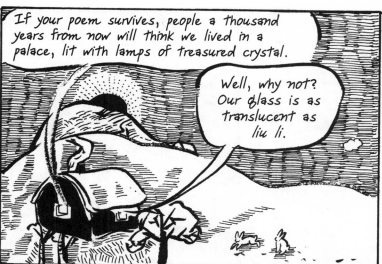

If your poem survives, people a thousand years from now will think we lived in a palace, lit with lamps of treasured crystal.

Well, why not? Our glass is as translucent as *liu li*.

Haiya, we're so poor, and you're still making merry.

If one is happy, one doesn't feel the poverty.

And, Brother, aren't we a happy pair?

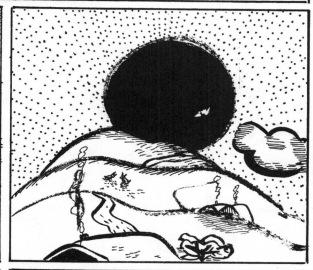

By the fall of 1957, eight years had passed under the auspices of the People's Republic of China.

Mrao!

That's right, Chairman Mao.

They had lived through a period of "transition to Socialism," but they saw no improvement in their lives.

Chairman Mao!

They were veterans of China's First Five-Year Plan (1953–57), a move to achieve industrialization, collectivization of agriculture, and political centralization.

They survived the "Let a Hundred Flowers Bloom" campaign when intellectuals were encouraged by Communist leaders to criticize the state.

There is total lack of freedom under the Chinese Communist Party.

There should be a four-year transitional government.

By the end of the year, those who had raised their voices against the government were put in prison, tortured or killed.

That autumn of 1957, their luck changed.

Hey, we've got a letter from Shenyang, written by my Lingzi and your Jun.

Our daughters?

As soon as they were old enough, the girls had gone to the city in search of work. They were hired as shop clerks.

Where will we sleep tonight, Jun?

We don't even own a single piece of bedding . . .

"We've established ourselves, married and are doing passably well. We have our own apartments and a bit of savings . . .

"Come and live with us. It'll be a little tight but we both have kids who need watching.

The money we'll be able to save on babysitting will cover your food and expenses."

What do you think, Eldest Brother?

All Father could do was weep.

The village authorities were happy to release the men and their wives, because they had grown old and were even more useless.

In Shenyang, Second Uncle went to work for a glass factory as an accountant to unravel a decade of muddled ledgers.

Initially, his colleagues looked down on him, a man always dangling a cigarette between his teeth and burning holes in his clothes.

He looks more like a thief than an accountant.

But the better they got to know him, the more they liked and respected him.

Tell us more stories, Comrade Yang.

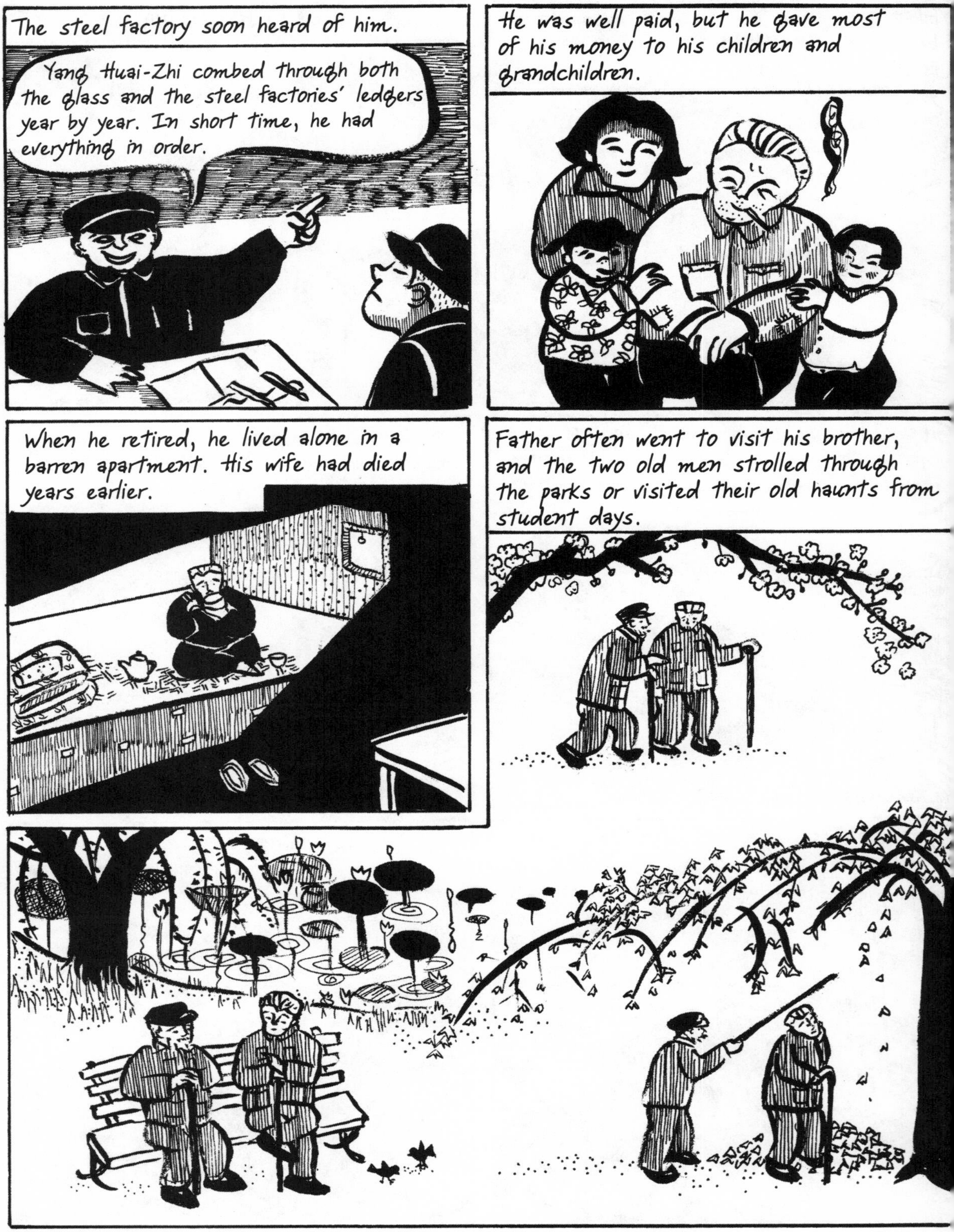
The steel factory soon heard of him.
Yang Huai-Zhi combed through both the glass and the steel factories' ledgers year by year. In short time, he had everything in order.
He was well paid, but he gave most of his money to his children and grandchildren.
When he retired, he lived alone in a barren apartment. His wife had died years earlier.
Father often went to visit his brother, and the two old men strolled through the parks or visited their old haunts from student days.

"Eldest Brother, your problem can be stated in one word. Greed. This is why you've made no progress in your meditation."

"Your nice clothes, your secretive outings for little delicacies and snacks."

"He's right."

"Was this around the time we moved to Japan and you were able to send money?"

"Yes, 1964. At the end of the famine, which is said to have taken more than thirty million lives."

Father would buy clothes for Second Uncle, but the man refused them. He did, however, accept gifts of sausages.

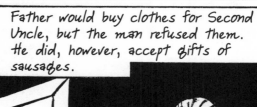

One spring day in 1965, Father found Second Uncle ill.

"Here, take my pillow and rest your back against the wall."

Father saw that the pillow was shiny with grease.

"I don't need the pillow. Don't make tea. You need to rest."

Only half of the lid to the teakettle remained. The spout was broken, as was the handle. The rims of the teacups were chipped.

You're here. I feel better already.

Two days later, Father went to see his brother again. Second Uncle had difficulty opening his eyes.

Who is it? Ah, Eldest Brother. Sit, sit ...

He struggled but could not get up.

Nearing home I grow more afraid

I dare not ask the man approaching

近鄉情更怯
不敢問來人

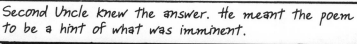

What did I recite?

That's the latter part of a poem by Song Zhiwen of the early Tang Dynasty.

Eldest Brother, I'm going home.

Huai-Zhi, you'll be all right.

You must rest.

Jun, go quickly to your dad. He won't last much longer.

Next day:

Uncle, my dad died last night. His body is at the hospital, awaiting cremation.

When Father pulled back the sheet, he saw that his brother's face was peaceful.

Tell me, Huai-Zhi, are you home? Are you truly in the palm of Buddha?

As he made his way back to his apartment, he remembered when he and his brother played together at the old brick kiln on the edge of the dunes.

Everything is as he wished.

His bedding will be burned. He did not want to leave evidence of his existence on Earth.

Baba, he did leave his excellent poems for us.

Mm . . . yes.

That evening:

That winter of 1948, when Grandfather and Youngest Aunt returned to Xinmin . . .

. . . they found their estate occupied by strangers.

This isn't your home. It belongs to the people!

They were put under surveillance by the neighborhood committee.

Were they mistreated?

I'm sure of it. Few escaped physical harm.

I am sure the Patriarch remained dignified.

They gave Grandfather the worst of the criminal labels: Capitalist.

资本家

Some of his former renters came to his defense.

This old man was good to people. He did not bully.

Sure, he used to be a big, rich businessman, but he's been retired for a long time.

We should downgrade his crime to Declining Capitalist.

No one mentioned executing him. Neither did they talk about labor reform camp.

They decided to cast him off his estate, making him homeless.

SCRAM!

But what happened to Youngest Aunt?

I don't know how she and Grandfather parted.

Perhaps he left, wanting to spare her the connection to a Capitalist?

They'll take away my teaching position if they find out I'm related to you.

I can't go to Shantuozi.

They tell me my wife is dead and Huai-Lian sent to labor camp.

I've had my fights with Eldest and Second Son. They blame me for giving the land to Huai-Lian, when I should have sold the land before the Communists came.

Even if I go to Shantuozi, I can no longer work the fields.

Maybe my eldest daughter will take me in. But she's deep in the countryside where life is harder.

Or my fourth son. He's gone to Shenyang now. What with his mechanical skills, it will be easy for him to find work.

You, gods, how did all of this come to pass?

Where did he go? How did he find food?

Maybe Yuan the Idiot took him to abandoned temples and begged food for him.

I could imagine Yuan a guardian to his former benefactor.

Oh, the Taoist beggar man who told the Patriarch to surrender earthly illusions.

SCRATCH

SCRATCH

Granddaddy, wear these. Long gowns represent the old society and will get you in trouble.

Yuan led Grandfather from one shelter . . .

. . . to another.

One day, Grandfather made his way to Shenyang, appearing at Fourth Uncle's new home.

You can't stay here, old man!

Didn't you used to call me Dad?

Did you not eat at my table?

Old man, you are a Capitalist. We cannot call you Father any longer.

Did I not shelter, feed, clothe and care for your old father along with your brother and his wife when they had no place to go? They lived with me for years.

Haii...

if you do not remember, then you are not human.

You and my family must draw a clear line between us.

I didn't come to see you. I came for my son.

Tell your dad not to come home. The old one is here.

Evening arrived.

He had not eaten in days. The same woman who had piously cooked pork for him on her husband's payday now offered him nothing. Not even water.

If you don't leave, I'll call the police.

Even if the woman wants nothing to do with me, surely my son will take me in.

Dad, of course, you can live with us.

But if he cannot shelter me, perhaps he can give me a bit of money to stave off this hunger.

Granddaddy, you have found a frozen snake and warmed it against your heart. It revived and bit you.

For some time, no one heard from him. He was like a person who had fallen into a fast-flowing river, where occasionally someone would see an arm emerge from the foam.

Farther down the river someone else would see a leg.

Grandfather appeared at the home of his eldest daughter and her husband in the countryside near Sijiazi in 1959.

229

It was during the famine that resulted from Mao's attempt to force rapid agricultural advances and industrialization, known as the Great Leap Forward.

I was born on Taiwan as people on the Mainland starved.

My eldest aunt, her husband and daughter made their escape out the back window.

When Grandfather found the house empty, he hobbled over to the neighbor's hut.

Have you seen my daughter?

Should be home. They're always home.

Grandfather reentered his daughter's home.

Nothing in the wok.

He was famished and had no choice but to go back to the neighbor. The peasant fed him.

I know they fled from me. If you have raised children, may you never reap disloyalty.

Some dried sorghum to take with you.

If my second daughter were still alive, she would not have mistreated me.

She was ever gentle, her voice melodic.

She would have filled my belly.

She would have sheltered me.

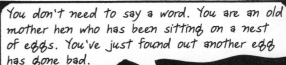

Yuan, I don't want to go on living.

Granddaddy, these trials are put in our way to temper us, to make us ready for the Great Western Paradise.

Why didn't your father find Grandfather?

He and his family could barely keep alive.

My money didn't reach them until after the famine had come to an end.

And how would Father find one wandering beggar in the upheaval?

Also, friends and kinsmen may not have wanted to say they saw him but didn't help him.

232

Some years after the Communist takeover, Fourth Uncle heard about the opening of a new factory in Huhehaote, in the Inner Mongolia Autonomous Region of the People's Republic of China.

It would be best to be as far away as possible from people who know our background.

The old man will have a tough time finding us here. It takes a train ride from Shenyang to Beijing and then a transfer. A three-day trip.

But Grandfather turned up at Fourth Uncle's door in Huhehaote during the winter of 1960 at the height of the famine.

Who gave you our address? We moved so far away and you still find us.

We don't have food enough for ourselves.

I've got my own grain ration tickets. I won't be a burden to you.

Your status is unclean. You will ruin us all.

But they couldn't very well push him into the night. They gave him the cold end of the kang, far from the stove. His bedding was inadequate.

In the morning, Grandfather was feverish and could not get to his feet.

...I have ration tickets...I have them...

He can't expire here, because we would have to report his death, and that will reveal our background.

...

Don't feel guilty about not doing your duty as a son. Think what will happen to our children. They won't get proper schooling.

He is old. He has enjoyed life. We can't sacrifice our happiness for him. We've got an application in to join the Communist Party.

Without membership, we will be third-class citizens. We won't get decent housing, or even good meat.

Yes, our future—everything—depends on getting into the party.

And besides, he isn't father to you alone. He's got other sons and daughters.

Buy a third-class ticket and send him back.

Who took care of Grandfather on his return journey? Who gave him food and water?

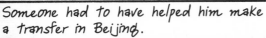

Someone had to have helped him make a transfer in Beijing.

He arrived in Shenyang on the morning of the third day.

Here's an address I found in his pocket.

The two railroad workers put him in a wheelbarrow and headed for the address.

Did Fourth Uncle put the address in his pocket?

Hmm . . . I think so.

Hei! Anyone named Yang living here?

Hei!

It was the first time Father had seen Grandfather after a dozen years of hardship.

Could it be Father? Dad! Dad!

Dad! It's me. Huai-Chao!

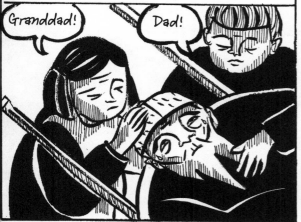
When my mother and my sister, Lingzi, heard his cries, they came running.

Grandad!

Dad!

Tears blinded Father, as he staggered to lift Grandfather up the flight of pitted, narrow stairs.

Grandfather was lucid. My mother boiled water to give Grandfather a sponge bath.

After putting him in fresh clothes, she settled him on the kang and fed him.

When your brother in Inner Monglia saw me, he said, "We've come so far and you still come to find us." Everyone's heart has changed. Only yours have not.

Why, what should we change into, Dad? We won't change. We'll always be the same.

Dad, rest easy and live with us. We'll take good care of you.

I have reached safety after all. I did not die alone on the road or among strangers.

?

This is your great grand-daughter. The older two are at school.

Ye-ye. Doesn't he have any toys to play with?

Grandfather's condition grew worse. At times, he dipped into delirium.

Dad, can you eat?

I don't want anything, Yong-Qin. No need to waste food on me. There is precious little to go around.

I'm going today.

Father sat by Grandfather's bedside, listening for his whispered words.

Was it because we did something wrong? Have we done something bad to deserve this?

I gave my best to my children.

How come I've had to suffer like this?

Oh, Heaven, bring them misery to be their teacher!

Dad, dear Dad, we are Buddhists and Taoists. We must not resent anyone. Our suffering is part of the plan.

Dad, you must not be attached to this world. Do not become attached even to your anger.

This world does not belong to us. The pain is beyond our control. So is the joy.

If you bear hatred in your heart, you will not be able to reach the Western Paradise.

240

Forget sorrow. Forget sorrow, Dad. Do you understand?

Dad, wash away your anger. Amituofuo. Amituofuo. You must recite the sutra. Only then will bodhisattvas guide you to nirvana.

Amituofuo. Don't think of the pain. Think only of Buddha.

People like us—we should not be destroyed by fire like the poor.

To Father's sorrow, he realized the Patriarch, a man who had fervently practiced Buddhism his entire life, had not relinquished the trappings of this world.

Release yourself from the wheel of incarnation. Do not return this way.

Forget sorrow. Forgive your children. Forgive the world.

On a spring morning, in an old public cemetery, south of Shenyang, the family buried the Patriarch in a casket constructed hastily from old shipping crates from the Soviet Union.

There was no crashing of cymbals, whining of trumpets, no incense, wine and food, as in yesteryear, to send off the soul of the dead.

We are men and women who deeply respect the past.

We will do nothing to disrupt the harmony of the universe and shame ourselves before our ancestors.

He placed a single brick at the foot of the grave mound to mark it.

He stared into the distance.

One day, when things get better, I'll take Dad back to old Granddaddy Hill.

My father did believe he would one day be able to reunite Grandfather with Grandmother.

But the Communist government demolished the Shenyang public cemetery—a sacrilege.

They did not notify the families to retrieve the bones.

In the end, it wouldn't have mattered. The ancestral burial ground was also cleared and the bones tossed into the wilderness of Badaohaodao, where, in the days of old, the homeless were buried.

My sister, one Qing Ming Festival, walked to the top of Old Granddaddy Hill, where houses of peasants has sprung up.

She burned spirit money to supply the ancestors with wealth in the afterlife. She bowed three times in the direction where the graves once stood.

2009: A couple of years ago, kinsmen contacted Baba by telephone after years of silence.

Baba learned that his father, Yang Huai-Chao, on returning from his customary morning stroll on the morning of May 20, 1993, asked Lingzi, his daughter, to prepare his funeral clothes.

Yang Huai-Chao sat on the kang in meditation. In the early evening, he stopped breathing.

His body remained upright.

The family did not disturb him. Peace would allow his spirit a clean break from the world.

They sat with his body for eight hours, then applied hot towels to put his stiffened body into his new clothes.

After Baba received this profound news, he came seeking my mother and me.

244

He burst into sobs as he retold the story of his father's death.

It was a sadness flooded with joy.

My father, after so much suffering and loss—after a life of selfishness and long struggle to be rid of desires—attained enlightenment.

According to his wishes, Yang Huai-Chao's granddaughters took his ashes in 2001 to holy Wutai Mountain.

His wife's ashes—she had preceded him in death—were buried with him between two pines on Yuanzhao Temple grounds.

Baba, musing on Yuan the Idiot's prognostication, said one evening, "I'm Crane Boy and I will return to the heavenly realm, leaving nothing, returning to the great Nothingness."

Hey, Baba, you're not going to fly off anywhere and leave your daughter behind!

Don't worry, you and your mom can join me in your own time.

In the process of writing this ancestral tale, I have tried to write sorrow out of Baba's life.

And in giving voice to Baba by carrying his stories out into the world, I have discovered the strength of my own voice.

Some years after the publication of my first illustrated adult book and more than a decade into my creative life, I awoke one morning to my soul somersaulting.

I realized I no longer lived in fear. By the time I began writing children's books, my stalker had found more interesting prey.

I thank heaven above for life's jagged path, without which I would never learn about solitude and patience.

You're wondering about the jade bi. Yes, it is the ancient jade from the Zhou Dynasty.

Baba gave it to me. He said I've grown strong.

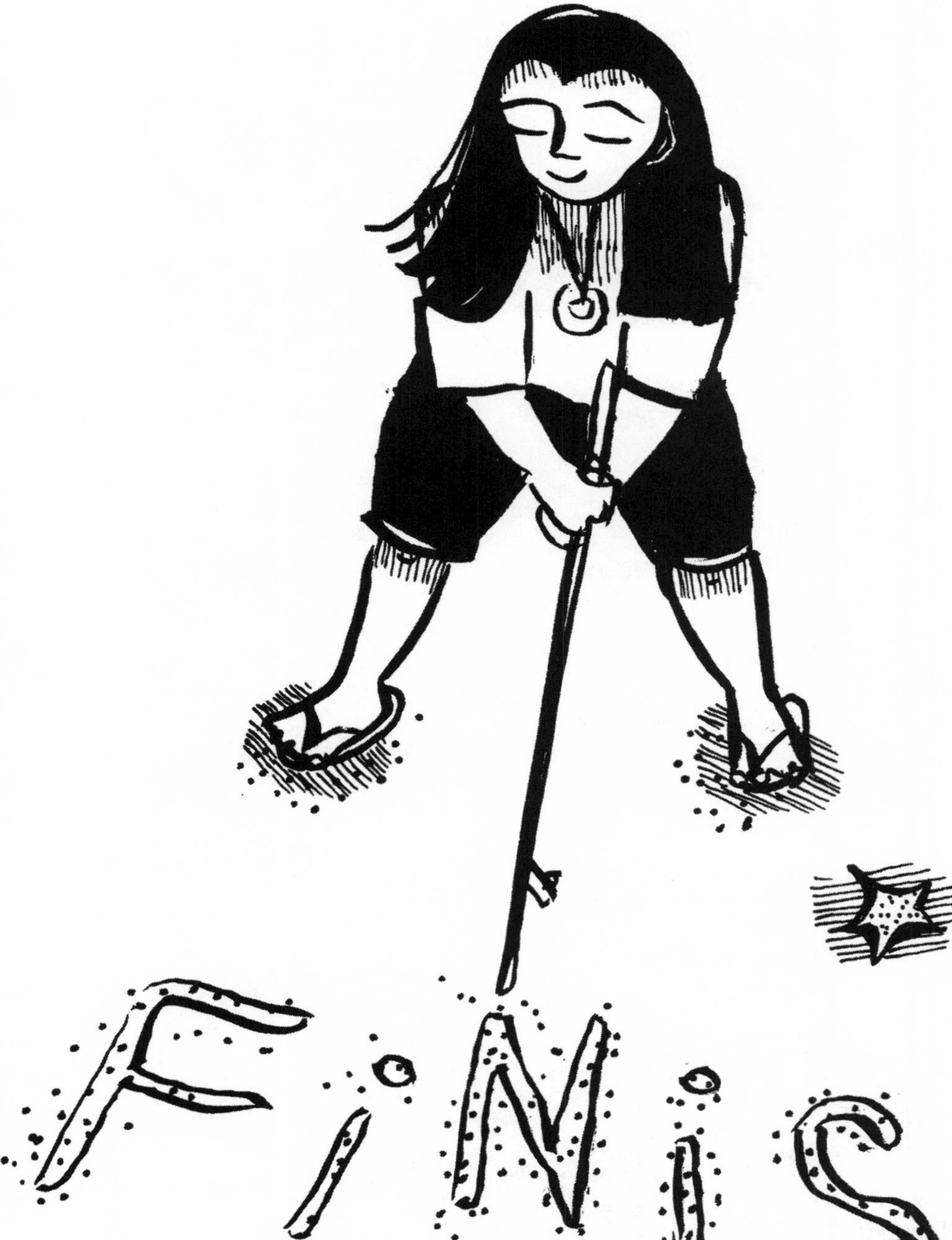
FiNiS

Bouquets of blessings
to consummate editor
Alane Salierno Mason,
who nudged me toward
the comics format.
My creative life owes
its renaissance
to you.

Thank You,
Deborah Warren,
for engendering
happiness and
humanity . . .

. . . and Denise Scarfi
for the countless tasks
you carry out
to make the
world go round.

In loving recognition of my grandmother Liu Yong-Qin,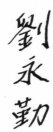

and my mother, Lin Laning.

I do not forget you uphold more than half the sky.